THE TESTIMONY OF A YOUTH

A STORY OF THE GRACE OF GOD
TOWARD A MAN

by
AYODEJI DAVID OLUSANMI

baruchpublishing.com

Copyright

The Testimony of a Youth
A Story of the Grace of God toward a Man
by Ayodeji David Olusnmi

Copyright © 2012 by Ayodeji David Olusanmi

ISBN: 978-1-62050-808-4

Contact Copyright Holder at

Ayodeji D. Olusanmi
Baruch Publishing
152 Oval Road North
Dagenham, Essex
RM10 9EH
England
info@baruchpublishing.com

This book was first published in 2010 by
Holy Fire Publishing and republished by
BARUCH PUBLISHING in 2012.

All rights reserved. No part of this publication may be reproduced, stored in a retrieval system, or transmitted in any form or by any means, electronic, mechanical, photocopying, recording, or otherwise, without the prior written permission of the publisher.

Unless otherwise noted, all Scriptures are taken from the Holy Bible, King James Version, which is in the public domain.

Scripture quotations marked NLT are taken from the Holy Bible, New Living Translation, copyright 1996, 2004. Used by permission of Tyndale House Publishers, Inc., Wheaton, Illinois 60189. All rights reserved.

Scripture quotations marked AMP are taken from the Amplified Bible, Copyright © 1954, 1958, 1962, 1964, 1965, 1987 by The Lockman Foundation. Used by permission.

Testimonial

This is a unique Christian Book in many ways. It has a unique audience Christian youth but is applicable to all Christians of all ages. Written by a youth – a young old man who has been there and seen it, experienced it, and now is burning for the Lord Jesus Christ.

It is also a special Christian book because it talks about the whole Christian character. This knowledge is necessary and important as we journey towards heaven. A so called Christian without christlikeness is still an instrument in the hand of devil no matter how religious he might appear. This book addresses contemporary issues which are over looked in most Christian books but are mandatory ingredients for becoming a giant and a vessel of honour in the hand of almighty God. Finally, I recommend this book to all Christian youths, parents, ministers in charge of youth ministry, children's ministries, and youth sunday school classes to read this book and your life will never be the same again, in Jesus' name. Amen

~ Pastor David B. Rufai

Dedication

*I dedicate this book to my wonderful Saviour
Jesus Christ, the Father of lights,
who saved and delivered me
from the power of darkness
and translated me
into His marvellous Kingdom.*

Thank You, my Lord.

Acknowledgments

I appreciate my parents, Mr and Mrs Ilesanmi, for their love and great support. Aside from God's grace, this great piece would not have been possible; thanks so much for being there when I needed you most. I am eternally grateful to God for the kind of biological brothers and sisters He gave me; you are all greatly beloved.

I also appreciate all authors whose books, tapes and biographies over time have trained and taught me. I am especially grateful to men like Dr. D .K. Olukoya, General Overseer of Mountain of Fire Miracles Ministries, a man amongst men. Though young, his great achievements are like those of a veteran, a pastor amongst pastors and a deliverance minister indeed! His ministry opened my eyes to the undoubted reality and genuineness of spiritual warfare.

I appreciate Pastor E. A Adeboye, whose in depth teaching of holiness made me see my need for holiness, without which no man can see the Lord. I gained also from his life of humility.

I cannot leave out Kenneth E Hagin (blessed memory), whose word of faith did not only open my eyes to the reality of having faith in God but whose deep scriptural insight keeps amazing me. George Müller's (blessed memory) drastic faith in God enabled me to see that the integrity of God can be upheld by the power of prayer. When I read such scriptures as Mark 11:23-24 and 1 Thess. 5:17, I can't help

Acknowledgments

but think of George Müller. I saw in him longsuffering, patience, obedience and total reliance on God. I praise God for these lives, as their lives and achievements are a challenge to me and a catalyst that continually makes me press on more ardently.

Finally, my heart goes out to the pastorate and the leadership of my local church, Mountain of Fire Miracles Ministries, Dagenham Branch. I also want to say how much I appreciate Lady Evangelist, Ayodele Alese, whose intimacy with the Lord has been a challenge and a blessing to me. Thanks also to those who proofread this book. May God richly bless you all.

Foreword

Youth are the leaders of tomorrow. They are the strong pillars in the house of God and in society. For a leader to make an impact in the house of God and society he must be a role model and have a visible testimony: a structure can stand firm only when the foundation and the pillar hold together. I, therefore, use this avenue to remind and encourage all church leaders, pastors and youth coordinators to train up every child placed under their supervision in the way he should go and when he is old he will not depart from it. It is only when a child is doing the will of God and working in His ways that he can make an impact in the church of God and in the society where he finds himself. A child who does the will of God will be useful to himself, and, in the church of God, will undoubtedly have a godly testimony.

In this book, "THE TESTIMONY OF A YOUTH" brother Ayodeji David Olusanmi has taken time to give us different testimonies ranging from personal purity to diligence. I, therefore, give you my word that this book is informative, educative and a "must" read for all pastors, church leaders, social workers, parents, counselors, youth coordinators and all youth.

Thanks and God bless you as you read and digest every chapter of this book.

~ Pastor (Mrs) Ipinmoroti Esther Omotayo Youth Ministry, Mountain Of Fire and Miracles Ministries.

Preface

One of the men I thank God for bringing across my path, said some words to me that were few but deep. I think they best describe the mystery of testimony. Many in churches today think of testimony as a waste of time, many see it as irrelevant, but God sees it as a deliverance tool. Remember we overcame Satan by the blood of the Lamb and by the words of our *testimony*. So friends, I appeal to you in the name of our Lord Jesus Christ that whenever you are anywhere and testimonies are being shared, please be sensitive enough to know what God is saying to you. Here are the words of Bishop David O Oyedepo on testimony:

> "Every time you listen to a testimony, try to grab the message the testimony is conveying; each testimony represents the unveiling of divine secrets to your blessing, every testimony is an unveiling of secrets that will lead to your divine destiny. Testimonies are prophetic arrows that will bring down another Goliath when the process is understood. Ps. 119:144 "**The righteousness of thy testimonies is everlasting: give me understanding, and I shall live.**" That means the validity of your testimony is everlasting, it will be repeated over and over again and again and again from everlasting to everlasting. Let me understand your testimony so I can have it repeated in my life." (Second service, Canaan land, Ota. Nigeria 30/05/2010).

Preface

It is therefore important to stress that testimonies represent acts of humanity's experiences of God. If you would like to experience God, then you must be ready to do what others did which enabled them to encounter Him.

Of a truth, experiencing God is in the doing. Mary, the mother of our Lord Jesus Christ, told the servants at the wedding in Canaan about our Lord Jesus Christ, she said "…Whatsoever he saith unto you, do it …" (John 2:5). And truly Jesus spoke to them and they did what He said and received their testimony; their water was turned to wine.

The Egyptians also experienced God because of something they did. When the famine began, they cried unto their king, Pharaoh, for bread, and he said "…Go unto Joseph; what he saith to you, do…" (Gen 41: 55). They did what Joseph said and they experienced God's deliverance.

So friends, experiencing God is not as difficult as you think; obey Him, then you will see Him working on your behalf. Read thoroughly and learn from this testimony then put the lessons into practice and watch God as He works deliverance for you.

Contents

Dedication V
Acknowledgments VII
Foreword IX
Preface XI
Introduction 1

   1- Personal Testimony 5
   2- Testimony of Integrity 19
   3- Testimony of the Fear of the Lord 33
   4- Testimony of Purity 41
   5. Testimony of Vision 51
   6- Testimony of Diligence 61
   7- Can I Have My Dad, Please? 67
   8- Testimony of Stewardship 73
   9- Scriptures for Meditation 79
   10- Christ in View 85

A Prayer for the Youth 91
Prayer Points 95
Prayer for Salvation 99
Prayer for Baptism in the Holy Ghost 101

Introduction

The elders have a saying that "the young shall grow." David spoke along this line when he said in Psalm 37:25 that, "I have been young and now am old...." This tells me that, truly, the young do grow. However, it is not enough just to grow old; we should all desire the old age that is blessed with the goodness of God. You know the Bible says something wonderful about Abraham, it says that, "...Abraham was old and well stricken in age and the Lord had blessed Abraham in **ALL** things..." (Gen 24:1).

What happened to Abraham was not something that *just* happened to him by chance; his experiences comprised the consequences of his obedience to divine instructions. He would certainly not have been blessed in **all** things by the Lord if he had not done certain things. It is therefore mandatory for anyone who desires to end up like Abraham to do the works of Abraham (See John 8:39).

Most often we sing "Abraham's blessings are mine...." But you know that if you do not do the works of Abraham you will never experience his blessings! So any young people that desire an Abrahamic testimony must be ready to work his works and walk his walk!

Seed and harvest time will never cease; if any youth desires a future like that of Abraham then he must begin to put some things in place, "...remember **now** thy Creator in the days of thy youth..." (Eccles 12:1).

The quality of life one would live later in life is a product of how one lived while young; hence for any youth to really shine in life there are some testimonies the individual must have.

This book will expand more on these testimonies. The saints of old had the same testimony and most of their achievements are still challenging **us to**day.

As a youth you will do well to ensure you have these testimonies.

As a parent make sure the riches you are laying up for your children, biological or adopted, are not uncertain riches but a good heritage of godly testimonies.

As a youth leader, teach it to the flock over which the Holy Spirit has made you overseer.

As a pastor ensure that you show everyone in the sphere of your influence the unsearchable benefit of a life with godly testimony. "PILLARS OF DESTINY" is what I call them and only upon these pillars can a lasting destiny be built. We want to build to last.

Remember that, when you are gone, the youth are the ones that will take over, hence it is compulsory that we, "TRAIN UP A CHILD IN THE WAY HE SHOULD GO: AND WHEN HE IS OLD, HE WILL NOT DEPART FROM IT" (Proverbs 22:6).

REMEMBER [earnestly] also your Creator [that you are not your own, but His property now] in the days of your youth, before the evil days come or the years draw near when you will say [of physical pleasures], I have no enjoyment in them. (Ecclesiastes 12:1 Amplified Bible)

1

Personal Testimony

Muller and Jacob

The story of my life brings to mind stories of men in biblical days, one of which is Jacob, who later became Israel. And in contemporary times, one person my testimony reminds me of is, German born, George Muller—a man whose life and faith demonstration have impacted me greatly.

Jacob was the third link in God's plan to start a nation from Abraham. Even before Abram was born God had already promised that His plan would be worked out through Jacob. It was recorded in the Bible that God said, **"…Jacob have I loved, but Esau have I hated…"** (Roman 9:13).

Looking closely into the life of Jacob, one sees that three stages characterized his life. First, during the initial stage of his life he demonstrated deception. Second, upon his encounter with God he demonstrated rugged determination, and the last stage of his life was marked by a high level of spiritual sensitivity (See Genesis 25:32 & 46).

George Muller had a similar experience. He was born in Kroppenstaedt, a town in the border district in Saxony-Anhalt, Germany. He had a terrible life marked by gross immorality; he lacked integrity and rebelled against God. His father gave him a religious education so he could get a job as a clergyman, not because he wanted him to serve God, but because it would enable him to give his parents assistance later in their lives.

He lived such an immoral life that when he lost his mother, he felt no remorse. He went that very night on an alcoholic spree. He must have drunk himself into a stupor, but as God would have it, at the age of 20 he met a friend, and that friend brought George Muller to a prayer meeting where they read the Bible, worshiped God in praises, and read a sermon. There God began a work of grace in his life. The great joy that resulted was far superior to that of the pleasures of sin.

George Muller, later became a traveling evangelist and it was known that he was a man of prayer and the word of God. He constantly meditated. All he achieved for God was by prayer, he never solicited money but went on his knees and believed that God would supply all his needs according to His riches in glory by Christ Jesus. And he experienced just that. The money came when needed. There was usually no excess but what was given was sufficient for the present need! He began caring for orphans and built orphanages in Bristol, England.

Reading about him brings great challenge and comfort to my soul because I am fully aware that He who began a good work in me will perfect it.

A Child is Born

I was born in Ibadan, Nigeria into a Christian-religious family. I was raised by my mother and her mother. My father had travelled abroad to the United Kingdom when I was about six years old, so most of my childhood was spent with my grandmother and my mother.

We had always gone to church, though never really experienced the reality of it. I went just because that was what we believed and it was fun because I often caught up with my friends. Though my grandmother was a praying mother, I often at that time thought within me she was going through unnecessary stress and wondered why she would and could pray that long. However, I now understand better! I had also a stepsister that seemed to be serious with the Lord and she would have her friend talk with me about the salvation plan of God for man through Jesus Christ. However, I rejected and made fun of them. I saw my sister's friend as a fool, and thought he was missing out on the enjoyment of life. I never knew that the devil had blinded my mind.

As at this time I was now a grown teenager and in secondary school. In school, I met friends who introduced me to alcohol, cigarettes and immorality. It was a boarding school so we were not under the supervision of our parents. Friday night we had a custom of escaping from the school premises in order to satisfy our fleshly lusts. On one occasion we were caught and were suspended from the school for two weeks, all this never moved me. I thought it was a normal way of life.

Study Abroad

I finally graduated from secondary school in the year 2002. Upon graduation I had no desire to study in my country. I proposed in my heart I would travel abroad to get my university education and I was specifically interested in the United Kingdom, because that was the country in which my parents now resided (my mother at this point had left Nigeria to join my father in the UK).

I told my parents of my plans and they agreed. I was very happy and I made all necessary application. I was called for an interview at the British High Commission in Lagos. My application was refused, and I felt terribly bad. Then I ran into a friend; though older than me he took me as his protégé. I explained my predicament to him and he took me to an herbalist. The herbalist gave me some assurance that the charm he gave would work. I used it as prescribed and made a fresh application. I was again refused; in fact, I was given less time to explain myself. I called the herbalist and he gave excuses. I lost hope in him.

I Fasted and Prayed

However, I remembered that my guardian was a fervent Christian and a wonderful woman. I met her and explained my situation to her, though I never told her about the herbalist, I just mentioned my desire to travel and she gave me a recommendation letter to me for her pastor. I met the pastor and he counselled my friend and me (I went with a friend that was also seeking a visa to travel).

The pastor said we would have to submit ourselves for a deliverance praying and fasting programme for which the ministry was well known. Mountain of Fire and Miracle Ministries is a deliverance ministry and, as the pastor instructed, we obeyed. It was a dry fast—no water, no food, for three days. I again made a fresh application, and to my surprise I was told to leave my document and wait for a reply because they wanted to validate my documents. I went home and after a couple of months I received a call and an email saying that my visa had been approved. I was very happy. My friend, too, went for an interview and he was given his visa.

All this happened not because I had a relationship with God, neither was I born again, but because there was an invisible handwriting on the wall revealing my destiny to suit His own pre-destined plan. God has big hands!

My family was happy and when I informed my parents, they were happy too. I was eager to see my father, whom I had not seen for a very long time.

England, Here I Come!

September, 2004, I gained entrance to the United Kingdom. I enrolled immediately into the university. I started taking prerequisite courses toward a degree, and during the induction I met some Nigerian students and we later became friends. We were told at the induction that students will be eligible for promotion and would spend six months instead of one year if they achieved high grades. I and my newly-found friends made this a goal to achieve and after the first semester we all received good marks and were promoted to year one.

The first year of our degree programme was interesting and challenging. Again, we made good grades and were promoted into year two. During this time, I remembered my mother's counsel. She often said to me, "I have not sent you to school in order for you to find a girlfriend. Face (focus on) your books! When you face them and pass (get good grades), girls will run after you." Such were the encouraging words of my mother.

Hell Broke Loose

Soon after this, hell was let loose on me without any logical explanation. I forgot my mother's advice and my friends and I lost the vision of excellence we had for our education. We engaged in all kinds of error; evil youthful exuberance took over, and we delved into gross immorality, examination malpractices, fraudulent activities, illegal driving---you name it we did it! My life was headed full-throttle down the wrong path. At this time, though, I had to quit smoking because, while in Nigeria, I got sick (I was vomiting blood), and the doctor told me that I would die the next time I smoked, so I was scared and stopped. He, however, did not warn me about alcohol and I continued, thinking it was okay. I drank it like water whenever we went out for parties.

Ready for Exams?

It was now time for examination—my friends and I had hardly read because we spent our time foolishly. You should be aware, at this time I had moved out of my parent's home and moved in with my friends. We had a house to ourselves; imagine what a rebellious child would do if he had a whole house to himself! He would set it on fire, and that was exactly what we did. We didn't light a literal fire but all we did made the house constantly busy and noisy. We listened to hip-hop music, and engaged in immorality and the fraudulent purchase of goods. When it was Sunday, I would drive down from where I lived with my friends in the northern part of London to Essex where my parents lived to pack some changes of clothes for the new week. The excuse for moving away from home was that it was closer to my school. Though it was true, the intention for this was to have more time for my sinful ways.

Now the result of the examinations came out, and we all did woefully. Some of us had to do a re-sit for the papers we had failed. We did not learn from what happened, neither did we study to pass, instead we looked for a way to purchase the examination papers beforehand. Sometimes we succeeded but when the results of the examination came out, we did not pass as we had expected.

Humorous Friend

During this time, we met a new Nigerian student whose father was a pastor, and I believe he had trained his son in the ways of the Lord. Our friendship with him influenced him to fall into a backslidden state. He had earlier told us he was a virgin and we made mockery of his purity. He seemed not to have enough moral strength, so he succumbed to our prompting and this got him off track and totally drenched in immorality. He now appeared to even run faster than us into evil.

He was very humorous and this specifically drew me closer to him as we both shared the same sense of humor. He was such a fellow that made jokes out of any frustrating situation. Nothing seemed to worry him. He appeared jovial but he had an excellent academic record just like us when we started. He eventually declined in his academic excellence and struggled to pass like we all did.

Gathering of Saints

He had a church service and some prayer meetings to which he was accustomed, and he would always invite us to these gatherings. I particularly went with him not because I wanted to learn anything, but because I loved his company. This reason soon changed when I attended a few meetings and saw beautiful girls. Now I always wanted to go, not mainly for his company but for the girls which I had seen. I did not like my parent's church because I was in a deadened spiritual state and also because a majority of the people were elderly.

Girls at the Gathering

The girls I saw at the meetings appeared to be fervent Christians but I knew little about their private lives. My friend's private life was nothing to write home about, so I assumed they were all the same, most especially because there was not much difference in their outfits compared to that of the girls I saw at the university. They were both dressed loosely and this often stimulated sexual and impure thoughts in me, but the leaders seemed different—a fire seemed to come out of their mouths as they ministered. I wondered how and where they learned what they were saying. They did not speak like my friend. Many a time I saw an attractive girl in those gatherings but I could not approach her; I did not know why. I was not exactly scared, but something beyond me kept me bound. Maybe it was the messages I heard. It burned in my heart and perhaps made me forget to flirt with the girls.

Though my humorous friend was in a backslidden state, nevertheless, he had a daily habit of reading a devotional book and a Bible and, afterward, he would mutter some strange words no one understood. I knew years later that those strange words are called "speaking in tongues." Though we respected his choice, we saw him as part of us because we engaged in the same sin.

How Forcible are Right Words!

It eventually became part of my schedule to go with him to the prayer meetings, but on one particular day, a brother named Solomon began to speak, I believe by the unction of the Holy Spirit. He made a statement that eventually led to my coming to the Lord. As he spoke he said, "You have been struggling in the world but come to Christ and He will give you peace." Though the statement was brief, it has remained with me from that day till now. The word pierced my heart. I was confused, struggling, yes I was, but with what? I could not specifically identify what I was struggling with. I thought everything was going well for me. I had access to buy whatever I wanted through various dubious means; I told myself all was well. But in spite of all this, within me all was not well for I was really disturbed and harbored great feelings of apprehension.

Stay Where You Are, London Metropolitan Police!

One morning the London Metropolitan Police raided our apartment in the northern part of London where I had been residing with my friends. They had a warrant to search the property as it was claimed that fraudulent activities were going on there. At this point, we had fought with our humorous friend and he'd left the previous night with his girlfriend. The police met four of us and eventually arrested myself and one of my other friends. The property was searched thoroughly and we were taken to the police station where all protocols were observed. They questioned us and we lied to them---pretending to tell them all we knew. Sometime in the evening we were released on bail to come back at various days while they carried out some investigation, because they had taken several computers from the property.

During this period, the police had visited my parent's house in order to confirm what I had said to them. This led to my parent's knowing what was going on and immediately they began ringing my mobile but I was out of reach. My father came to the police station but he was given wrong information. He was upset; my mother was crying. I eventually got through to them and I was commanded to come home immediately.

My mother questioned me but I lied to her. I told her I knew nothing about all that happened. She cried and I hate to see her cry. But, just the same, I was still unmoved. She told her pastor what had happened and had the pastor pray for me. The pastor prayed and counselled me and said we would observe a seven day fast and I should see him every day for prayers. I obeyed and went to him. He prayed with me and said that God would deliver me out of the snare in which I had put myself. Yes, I was a lawful captive! I never believed him when he said it but, as God would have it, on the morning of my third visit I received a call from my lawyer on the 7th of June 2007 saying that the police had decided to take no further action in the matter.

As soon as I got to the station, I saw the officer in charge of our case. He explained to me better what my lawyer had said over the phone, but he made some utterances that I still remember till today. He said, "I could see a glorious future ahead of you guys and I do not want to jeopardise it for you, because I could charge you if not for fraud, for aiding and handling stolen goods and I would get you convicted. But whatever I do will put your integrity at stake and no company will want to employ an ex-convict." Indeed, God had delivered me, a lawful captive. I was amazed, however, at his words; I could not understand him. Nevertheless I was happy. I called my mother and she rejoiced. I also called the pastor who had prayed for me and he further counselled me.

Again the words of Brother Solomon came to me like fire. It rang in my being. I thought of it for a while, but I soon forgot. Now I was free from the police. I, however, did not stop my sinful ways. I still engaged in fraud, though it was very minimal. Again, Brother Solomon's words came to me and I realize God had begun a work of grace in me.

Surrendered

Finally, in September 2007, I surrendered to Jesus Christ as my Lord and Saviour. I began reading a New Testament a wonderful sister had given me from the University Student Fellowship. I began reading the book of John and, to my amazement, found it interesting and I remember sending a text to one of my friends that, "this book of John, sweet ooo" meaning, "this book of John is so sweet." I again saw my need for a Saviour and understood that God had a plan for my life.

I was not able to stop all my sins at once; I still struggled with immorality. I did not renew my mind and, so long as I did not do this, I had challenges. I never believed I could live a day without committing an act of immorality. I had a girlfriend that satisfied most of my sexual desires. Ironically, she was a chorister in a backslidden state and the devil took advantage of her. We both needed a genuine touch from above.

Graduated at Last

During this time, we were now in our final year at the university and I was suspended for two years due to examination malpractice. However God had mercy on me and it was reduced to a year and I re-enrolled. While on suspension, I sought God and threw myself into His service while my humorous friend, too, re-dedicated his life to Christ, and to the glory of God only himself and I eventually graduated from the University. My other friends had challenges in passing their core modules, everything became stagnated, and they did not want to come to Christ. The invasion of police led to the scattering of every one of us. We grew a bit more focused. I now understood that God used it to shake us.

Mount Zion

At this time, I started attending the Mountain of Fire Miracle Ministries. It was a branch of this church I had been to in Nigeria where I prayed for my visa, so when I saw the branch of the church in the UK, I immediately joined and started worshiping. As their custom is, they had days in which deliverance services were held so I submitted myself for deliverance and I remember that during one of the services on a Saturday morning we were taught about the need for the Holy Spirit. The pastor ministered powerfully and, when it was time for the baptism and she went around laying hands on people to receive the gift and those whose hearts were open to the Holy Ghost received the baptism with the evidence of speaking in tongues. Immediately she got to me and laid her hands on me saying, "Speak those words now in Jesus' name" and I began muttering words I did not understand. I thought, "This is strange." I had received the Holy Ghost with the evidence of speaking in tongues!

I realized that my love for alcohol was gone and I cut myself off from every ungodly friend. I now made new friends in the church.

Israel Indeed

In February, 2008, I became serious with the Lord. My commitment took a deeper form after I read a book written by Rick Warren called *The Purpose Driven Life*. (I recommend this book for everyone). I remember saying to a friend that if she reads the book and she sees no changes in her life, I would refund her money. Now that is how good I know the book is! Get a copy. It is a must read!

By this time my relationship with my girlfriend was staggeringly uncomfortable. I knew we had to break up. I was prepared and God granted me the grace. We met to talk and I explained to her that we couldn't go on because it has a wrong foundation and, moreover, it ran contrary to God's will. She suggested we get married but I did not consent (You see, marriage is not the cure for adultery; neither is it for fornication. Discipline is the cure! And not just discipline but Spirit-empowered discipline!)

Though my emotions wanted to pull me back when I saw her crying, I refused to be ruled by them. I had come to know the truth and that truth would set me free if I complied with the truth I knew! I learned that we do not automatically become free because we know a truth. We must comply and work in accordance to the truth; then shall we be free indeed! It was challenging because I realized there was a soul-tie agreement due to our violation of the commandments of God. Sex before marriage is forbidden just as sex outside marriage is a sin. We had sinned; we had to pay for it. But I thank God the soul-tie covenant had been broken. During the deliverance service, I submitted myself to in the church (See 1 Corinthians 6), I explained everything to her. She cried and called me all sorts of names and said I was seeing someone else and I said, yes, I was seeing the Holy Spirit!

The sinful relationship finally was broken and God began to deal with me as a son as it is to this day. This is my sincere and faithful testimony, not that I have attained so as to think too highly of myself, but I keep my body under subjection. And my sufficiency is of God. I am not there yet, but I have committed myself and I am pressing toward the mark of the high calling God has placed upon my life.

I serve God faithfully to the best of my ability and knowledge as His minister at my local church. This I do with all gratitude and sincerity of heart.

This testimony is a proof that the saving power of Christ is still available to all that call upon him. Come to Christ now and He will set you free from every bondage. He did it for Jacob, George Muller, and for me. He will do better for you if you dare to come believing.

I discovered that testimonies are a powerful tool for evangelism because I remember sharing my testimony with a group of young adults during street evangelism. I told them what Christ did for me; how He delivered me from alcoholism and gross immorality. They were intrigued and their faces lit up. It seemed to me that they had never heard anything like this before and upon hearing it, their souls were opened for salvation. I prayed with them and they left.

Testimonies are meant to be shared, and, through them, God edifies, converts and delivers. Every testimony communicates a particular message and when we are able to understand it and put it to work; we will definitely get fruitful results.

GLORIOUS THINGS

It has been two years since the publishing of this book, I thank God for the great things that has happened as a result of it, most especially the testimonies it has produced in the life of those who have read it. To God alone be praised. This also opened to us speaking engagement at various conferences and I thank God for opening such doors of ministry.

We have also been privileged to published another book—*The Prayer That Works*. Our other works are also in progress. June 2010, I was introduced into the leadership of one of our branches in the Mountain of Fire Miracle Ministries where I currently serve as a branch coordinator. All these are due to the faithfulness of God. He opens each phases of our destiny as we follow him.

The following chapters that you are about to read spells out the testimony I believe an individual should posses—especially youth. It is my prayer that as you read the Lord will open the eyes of your understanding to see wondrous things.

2

Testimony of Integrity

The integrity of the upright shall guide them...
~ Proverbs 11:3

There are certain qualities and characteristics that a young individual must possess if the person desires in any way to fulfil their destiny and I strongly believe that one of these qualities is integrity.

Now what is integrity? The word integrity is from a Greek word known as "tome" which means *completeness, full, perfect, simplicity, uprightness* (morally), and *innocence*. Integrity has to do with trustworthiness. It involves knowing the truth and walking in it. However while we endeavour to walk in the truth, we may fall but scriptures bid us to rise again (See Proverbs 24:16).

Note this: when we say people have integrity this does not mean that they are always right, but they are individuals that will never defend their errors, neither will they rejoice in them. You see, someone can be innocently wrong.

Integrity will not only create a place for you in life but will, in addition, secure it for you because there is a great difference between being great and staying great. Many folks are great but few sustain their greatness. More important than being great is retaining the greatness bestowed upon us from God. Samson was great but he did not retain the greatness because he had no integrity. But Samuel, the prophet, became great and continued to be great until death. In fact it was recorded that everyone knew God had established him as a Prophet and a Judge. He was able to accomplish all this because he was a person of integrity.

Oh, how beautiful is expertise and education. I love education and I encourage everyone within the sphere of my influence to pursue education, study as much as they can. But, within me, I know that a human's destiny in the kingdom of God is not so much attached to educational background neither is it in the level of his expertise. Fulfilling the biblical destiny is a product of godly character, and integrity is part of this character.

Sadly, integrity is almost becoming extinct in the history of the church. In fact, anyone who mentions it is often labelled a fanatic, but in a real sense, any youth that embraces integrity will continually be guided into all truth.

Education without a love for, and a practice of, and a strong belief in integrity will certainly not amount to much because such individuals will or may never keep a good job. Employers are not just looking for the best brains but brains coupled with integrity. I have read and heard of how many people with great jobs have lost their positions due to lack of integrity. In fact, in the political sphere, one of the major reasons the ruling party was often not re-elected is because the citizens have lost confidence in them and when this happens it shows a lack of integrity in the government.

It is important for parents to know that it's not enough to send their children to school; they must ensure that they also possess godly qualities and character traits. Children should be taught to drop ungodly traits like stinginess, lack of empathy, and lying, to mention but a few, because if they grow up with them, it will affect the parents eventually. With all you are getting, develop integrity.

We have an account of a man named Job in the Bible; he was such a man who understood the benefit of integrity and we see him display this essential quality. See his testimony focuses on integrity. The Bible declares, "There was a man in the land of Uz, whose name was Job; and that man was perfect and upright, and one that feared God, and eschewed evil." (Job 1:1). Remember our definition of integrity, so from that definition and in comparison with what the Bible says of him you would agree with me that Job truly had integrity.

He was a man God could vouch for; see what God said about him. It is one thing for you to say something about yourself, or for people to say something about you, and entirely different when God says something about you. God cannot lie but humans can. "And the LORD said unto Satan, Hast thou considered my servant, Job, that there is none like him in the earth, a perfect and an upright man, one that feareth God, and escheweth (turns away from) evil?" (Job1:8).

So from Job 1:8 we see who Job was but let us take a deeper look into his life. The Bible says concerning him that, "...As I was in the days of my youth, when the secret (word) of God was upon my tabernacle (dwelling place or home)..." (Job 29:4).

Looking closely to this passage of Scripture we can see two things, one, the *time* integrity was found in him and, two, *how* he became a man of integrity. So we can say of Job that he had been a person of integrity since the days of his youth, and this was because he had access to the secret which also means counsel. In our day we would call it the ***word*** of God. Praise God we also have access to the word. Hence we can all have integrity.

Three people testified of Job's integrity: God, himself and his wife. We have already established what God said but now see what his wife said and what he said, too, of himself.

The Wife Said...

"Dost thou still retain thine integrity? Curse God, and die" (Job 2:9). You cannot retain what you never had, so you would agree with me that Job had integrity.

Even his reply showed that he was, indeed, a man of integrity, "**But he (Job) said unto her, Thou speakest as one of the foolish women speaketh. What? shall we receive good at the hand of God, and shall we not receive evil? In all this did not Job sin with his lips**" (Job 2:10). It takes integrity to not compromise even in the face of adversity.

Job was not such a fellow who looked for shortcuts, neither did he seek for the easy way out. In fact, he said of himself that, "**If a man die, shall he live again? all the days of my appointed time will I wait, till my change** come" (Job 14:14). You see, Job was simply saying, rather than compromise, it is better to die. He was not ready to tarnish his image; he held on to his integrity. In contrast, many young people of this generation seem to know little or nothing about integrity, so they do things without considering the repercussions. They act in whatever way they wish, rebel against authority and they call it human rights. What a shame! Teens and young adults are constantly looking for shortcuts; how to get rich quick, how to experience instant gratification, to mention but a few. And, in line with this, they do not want to wait on the Lord. They are constantly looking for the easy way out. Some of the things they do are not even fit to be mentioned. However, unknown to them, the devil uses all of these to set snares for them. Wait for your time. The servant that waits for his master shall be honoured.

Job Said Of Himself…

"God forbid that I should justify you: till I die I will not remove **mine integrity** from me" (Job 27:5).

"Let me be weighed in an even balance that God may know **mine integrity**" (Job 31:6).

I strongly believe that Job's wealth was as a result of his integrity, because the Bible says that Job was the greatest of all the men in the East during his time. He had a testimony of integrity and knew how to guard it. When we begin to realize the importance of integrity, we will do everything in our power to acquire, maintain and walk in it.

You see, when you begin to embezzle money to become rich or falsify records in order to be wealthy it automatically shows discontentment which is a result of lack of integrity. Sadly enough, this seems to be the everyday practice of a great many people of this generation. They engage in internet financial fraud (SCAM). If you are into this, stop now! Remember, *let him that steals steal no more but let him work with his hands so he may have to give to him that is in need* (Eph 4:28).

In the same way young girls also engage in every form of sexual immorality in order to get money. You see, selling your body for fun or even to raise money for a cause such as education is wrong. It is a sin. Stop now before it is too late. It reflects a lack of integrity. Learn to possess your body in honour and sanctification (1 Thess 4:4).

David was also one such person we find in the Bible who walked in integrity. Though he committed some atrocities, we, however do not read neither did we see him repeating such atrocities. This he showed in the twelfth chapter of the second book of Samuel when Nathan, the prophet, came to him to confront him of his evil deed against Uriah. David did not deny it, he accepted his fault and fell on his face asking God for mercy.

2 Samuel 12:7-10 & 13

⁷And Nathan said to David, Thou art the man. Thus saith the LORD God of Israel, 'I anointed thee king over Israel, and I delivered thee out of the hand of Saul;

⁸'And I gave thee thy master's house, and thy master's wives into thy bosom, and gave thee the house

of Israel and of Judah; and if that had been too little, I would moreover have given unto thee such and such things.

⁹'Wherefore hast thou despised the commandment of the LORD, to do evil in his sight? thou hast killed Uriah the Hittite with the sword, and hast taken his wife to be thy wife, and hast slain him with the sword of the children of Ammon.

¹⁰'Now therefore the sword shall never depart from thine house; because thou hast despised me, and hast taken the wife of Uriah the Hittite to be thy wife.

¹³And David said unto Nathan, 'I have sinned against the LORD.' And Nathan said unto David, 'The LORD also hath put away thy sin; thou shalt not die....'

Another person we can see from the Bible who had a testimony of integrity is Abimelech. The king had taken Abraham's wife in the innocency of his heart. He acted wrongly because he received false information but God knew that King Abimelech had integrity. See what the Scriptures says of him.

Genesis 20:1-8 & 14

¹And Abraham journeyed from thence toward the south country, and dwelled between Kadesh and Shur, and sojourned in Gerar. ²And Abraham said of Sarah his wife, She is my sister: and Abimelech king of Gerar sent, and took Sarah.

³But God came to Abimelech in a dream by night, and said to him, Behold, thou art but a dead man,

for the woman which thou hast taken; for she is a man's wife.

⁴But Abimelech had not come near her: and he said, LORD, wilt thou slay also a righteous nation?

⁵Said he not unto me, She is my sister? and she, even she herself said, He is my brother: in the integrity of my heart and innocency of my hands have I done this.

⁶And God said unto him in a dream, Yea, I know that thou didst this in the integrity of thy heart; for I also withheld thee from sinning against me: therefore suffered I thee not to touch her.

⁷Now therefore restore the man his wife; for he is a prophet, and he shall pray for thee, and thou shalt live: and if thou restore her not, know thou that thou shalt surely die, thou, and all that are thine.

⁸Therefore Abimelech rose early in the morning, and called all his servants, and told all these things in their ears: and the men were sore afraid.

¹⁴And Abimelech took sheep, and oxen, and men servants, and women servants, and gave them unto Abraham, and restored him Sarah his wife.

Notice that verse fourteen says that Abimelech, *"...gave unto Abraham and restored* (God told him to restore, he did exactly just that, he restored!) *him Sarah his wife."* You see sometimes to prove your integrity you may have to do restitution. Restitution is an act of repentance and a sign of integrity. However, every restitution demands thorough counsel.

Another man that comes to mind is the, apostle, Paul. Looking closely at all the epistles which he wrote to the churches, one would conclude that he was a man of integrity. From his letters both to Timothy and Titus you would see that Paul was a man that encouraged integrity; as a matter of fact, the job description of a bishop and elder as prescribed by the Holy Ghost through Paul to both Timothy and Titus respectively had integrity as its focus (See Titus 1 and 1 Timothy 3).

Paul, the apostle, was also a man that fought vigorously against anyone that exhibited any lack of integrity. To stop an indecent act, it must be fought. When folks decide to allow indecency, then it most often grows out of control.

Let us read the account of how Paul, the apostle, rebuked apostle, Peter, on the matter of integrity.

Galatians 2:11-14

[11]But when Peter was come to Antioch, I withstood him to the face (**you see Paul did not need to ask someone to confront Peter, he did it himself! Until you stand up and confront every form of ungodliness in the sphere of your** influence, it will certainly continue), because he was to be blamed.

[12]For before that certain came from James, he did eat with the Gentiles: but when they were come, he withdrew and separated himself, fearing them which were of the circumcision.

¹³And the other Jews dissembled likewise with him; insomuch that Barnabas also was carried away with their dissimulation.

¹⁴But when I saw that they walked not uprightly according to the truth of the gospel, I said unto Peter before them all, If thou, being a Jew, livest after the manner of Gentiles, and not as do the Jews, why compellest thou the Gentiles to live as do the Jews?

Peter had been eating with the uncircumcised gentiles but when the apostle, James, and other disciples came, Peter refused to eat again with the uncircumcised gentiles. Paul saw exactly what was occurring and he confronted Peter about his act of hypocrisy. Integrity can be costly but it is worth it, and, most often, you will be required to stand alone.

However, all believers must ensure that they maintain the integrity of the Kingdom of God. See what Paul wrote to Titus. In the book of Titus chapter 3 verse 8, it says, "This is a faithful saying, and these things I will that thou affirm constantly, that they (all, not just pastors, evangelists, apostles, teachers, bishops, Paul meant all believers!) which have believed in God might be careful to maintain good works (walk in integrity). These things are good and profitable unto men." (You see that it says unto men not unto God. We need to realize that obeying God is for our benefit. The Psalmist said it is good for me to draw near to God [Ps 73:28]. When you walk in integrity it is to your advantage; it goes into your record, not your neighbour's).

Samuel, The Prophet

Samuel was also another man of integrity; none of his words ever fell to the ground! (1 Sam 3:19). Why? Because he always did what he said and said what he did. The young folks of this generation tend to be entirely different.

We've heard testimonies about the lives Christians were leading some 30-40 years ago. We were told that if a Christian was caught in adultery he would cry and almost kill himself (that is, genuinely cry for forgiveness and repentance). But what we see now in the lives of many a 'Christian' is totally different. They see nothing wrong in lying; they drink fornication and gulp adultery like water. Alcohol consumption is at its peak! And when you try to show them from the Scripture that it is wrong, you will hear them say, "Jesus turned water to wine, you know, and the Bible did not say if it was alcoholic or not, in fact the Bible only *says* do not be drunk in excess." I have actually had someone say to me that, "if Jesus never wanted us to drink alcohol, why did he change water to alcohol? Why didn't He leave it as water?" My heart bleeds when I hear people speak this way because I know that the devil has blinded their minds. They forget that this same alcohol will destroy them if they do not quit drinking it. Someone called it a "sin-drenched world." Perfect description!

We also heard that employers were always looking to employ Christians in their organisations because the Christians in those days had a testimony of integrity; but what we see happening today contrasts with this. The news is filled with stories of pastors, televangelists or prophets stealing money, not to mention some that are being locked up in prison for various other atrocities committed. I plead with you to repent at this point and turn from your sinful way, for the wages of sin is death!

We see a genuine display of integrity in the life of Samuel. He made a bold declaration in First Samuel, chapter 12, that few people are able to make in this day and age:

1 Sam 12:2-4

²And now, behold, the king walketh before you: and I am old and grayheaded; and, behold, my sons are with you: and I have walked before you **from my childhood** unto this day.

³Behold, here I am: witness against me before the LORD, and before his anointed: whose ox have I taken? or whose ass have I taken? or whom have I defrauded? whom have I oppressed? or of whose hand have I received any bribe to blind mine eyes therewith? and I will restore it you.

⁴And they said, Thou hast not defrauded us, nor oppressed us, neither hast thou taken ought of any man's hand.

It will be prudent to note that by the time of this utterance, Samuel was already old but what he asked the people was not just concerning what is happening his old age but encompassed his entire life. Samuel was simply saying that ever since he was small, "...Whose ox or donkey have I stolen? Have I ever cheated any of you? Have I ever oppressed you? Have I ever taken a bribe and perverted justice? Tell me and I will make right whatever I have done wrong." (1 Sam 12:3 NLT).

Samuel, the prophet, had a testimony of integrity at his old age which he kept from his youth.

There is an adage that says, *"a child's future becomes easily predictable by his present behaviour."* This simply means that when you take a close look at any child and discover a behavioural habit in him, then you can predict the future of that child. The life Samuel, the prophet, lived was a product of how he had lived when he was young.

It is necessary to take note that all the individuals we have mentioned including Job, David, Paul and Samuel all had something in common which is God and His Word.

JOB: Eschewing evil from his youth

As I was in the days of my youth, when the secret of God was upon my tabernacle (Job 29:4).

DAVID: Shepherd boy turned king

Wherewithal shall a young man cleanse his way? by taking heed thereto according to thy word. Thy word have I hid in mine heart, that I might not sin against thee. Thou art my portion, O LORD: I have said that I would keep thy words (Psalm 119:9, 11 & 5).

PAUL: Student of the Word

Study to shew thyself approved unto God, a workman that needeth not to be ashamed, rightly dividing the word of truth. The cloke that I left at Troas with Carpus, when thou comest, bring with thee, and the books, but especially the parchments. (2 Timothy 2:15; 4:13)

SAMUEL: Listener to God

And the LORD appeared again in Shiloh: for the LORD revealed himself to Samuel in Shiloh by the word of the LORD. (1 Samuel 3:21)

Without God and His word a genuine Spirit-driven integrity can never be experienced! Stay close to the word. It is the source of life.

3

Testimony of the Fear of the Lord

And there shall come forth a rod out of the stem of Jesse, and a Branch shall grow out of his roots: And the spirit of the LORD shall rest upon him, the spirit of wisdom and understanding, the spirit of counsel and might, the spirit of knowledge and (the spirit) of the fear of the LORD.

~ Isaiah 11:1-2

The above Bible passage was a prophecy given about our Lord Jesus Christ; and if you will look closely to this verse there are many things we can see. If you count those spirits or attitudes as related to Jesus Christ, you will find out that they are seven spirits, which stand for the perfect, life-restoring Spirit of the Lord. The number seven means perfect, completeness, finished and rest.

Pay close attention to the fact that the last spirit recorded among those spirits is the spirit of the fear of the Lord. Now, why did the spirit of the fear of the Lord have to be included among those seven spirits and why was it last? Firstly, if this spirit had not been included, the rest of the spirits would never be complete and we would have six spirits. Number six represents carnality, satan, flesh, idol, the beast, and manifestation of sin. This is to show us how vital is the spirit of the fear of the Lord.

Some people call it "the seal" and I agree with them. It is the spirit that sets a seal upon the other spirits which are recorded in Isaiah 11:1-2. Imagine running with a bottle without covering it; you will surely lose its contents by the time you get to your destination! Hence the spirit of the fear of the Lord is that spirit which makes us perfect and whole.

Secondly, I believe this spirit of the fear of the Lord had to be included because it is that spirit which makes our spiritual worship acceptable unto the Lord. Every saint of old that walked successfully with the Lord had this fear in them. Peter was brought back into the faith by the instrumentality of this spirit.

The spirit of the *fear* of the Lord; The *fear* here is not such a fear that grips you when there are terrible emergencies like earthquakes, tornadoes, and fire. The *fear* here is from the Greek word "yir-aw" which means "moral reverence." This occurs as a result of your love for Him which will make you desire to never disobey Him. The Amplified version of Isaiah chapter 11, verse 2, has a good description. It says, "….the Spirit of knowledge and of the **reverential and obedient** fear of the Lord…" The love of Christ constrains us not to live to self, but to Him.

Long Life

The Bible says that, "The fear of the LORD prolongeth days: but the years of the wicked shall be shortened..." (Proverbs 10:27). Almost everyone wants to live long and that is why some people are very much interested in healthy eating and exercise. All this is good, and I encourage it because the Bible says physical exercise has some profit (See 1 Tim 4:8). The truth, however, is that none of this will guarantee a long life, if you have no "fear of the Lord" inside of you. The Bible says, "...Children, obey your parents in the Lord: for this is right. Honour thy father and mother; which is the first commandment with promise; that it may be well with thee, and thou mayest live long on the earth..." (Eph 6:1-3). This passage clearly tells us what a young person should do if they so desire to live long. Honour the elders! Not go to the gym! (Though the gym is good).

Love and Fear

I once heard a pastor friend say that, "a **love** for the Lord **may** not keep you from sin but the **fear** of the Lord **will definitely** keep you from sin." He is partly right; the danger is that, partial truth like this can sometimes do more damage than a total lie. Let me explain.

The love for the Lord and the fear of the Lord go hand in hand. You see, it is like a bicycle. To get moving, you need the two wheels to function properly; if a wheel is damaged you will certainly not move ahead with your journey until you get it fixed! This I believe, can illustrate the necessity of both the love and fear of the Lord. When one of these is out of place then certainly our walk with Him is damaged. Are you carrying a damaged relationship with the Lord? We must love and fear Him.

It is one thing for you to say, "Oh how I love Jesus," but your actions may not correspond with what you confess. Your belief must be equal to your behaviour. The younger souls of this generation appear to love the Lord. They will act religious, but they also sometimes reject the power that could make them godly (2 Tim 3:5).

It is not enough to say you love the Lord; you must bring forth fruits that show you really mean what you are saying. "By their fruits ye shall know them" (Matt 7:20).

The fear of the Lord constitutes holy reverence. It amazes me how people get so attentive and dedicated when watching mundane television programmes and these same people come to church and do not mind disturbing others while the service is going on! Some even use their telephone, engaging in unnecessary conversation. You see, God will not bless your life through that service if that sort of conduct is occurring because it shows there is no godly and moral reverence for Him. The church needs to learn how to reverence the King if we expect Him to dwell in our midst every time we gather.

Fruitless Service

The Bible says that God, "...did not call the descendants of Jacob [**to a fruitless service**], saying, Seek Me for nothing (**there is always a blessing for every gathering of saints**) but I promised them a just reward. I, the Lord, speak righteousness (the truth--trustworthy, straightforward correspondence between **deeds** and **words**); I declare things that are right..." (Isaiah 45:19 AMP).

We need to realize that God is a good and just God! He gives unto everyone what each deserves. Whenever we gather in His presence it is for a reason. God did not call us together just to make fun; heaven does not joke! You may be a joker but God is not.

There is so much fruitless service going on now in this generation and it seems God is far away. The truth is, your service for God will be fruitless when your motives are not right. Nowadays people come to church from the altar of sin and lift up dirty hands, thinking they are holy; and this same people do not want to render a genuine repentance so they may be thoroughly washed and cleansed of their iniquity.

Imagine going to a church service expecting to hear from the throne of grace so as to find help in the time of need and all the speaker does for most of the time is to tell jokes! I ask you, if you were God would you bless such a gathering? God can only bless us as far as our obedience goes. The fullness of the blessing is a result of a fulfilled and complete obedience! Maybe you should have been reaping a better result than you are receiving now. Check your conduct. Your service to God must be rendered with godly fear. Then and only then shall you see fruits. Do not forget that, "...you cannot mock the justice of God. You will always harvest what you plant" (Gal 6:7 NLT).

The Fear of the Lord

> The fear of the Lord is to hate evil; it is to run away from everything and anything that appears evil (Prov 8:13; 1 Thess 5:22).

The testimony of the fear of the Lord is a direct product of the spirit of the fear of the Lord. A life without that spirit cannot experience that testimony. We must realize that it is naturally impossible for humans to fear--have moral reverence for--God due to our fallen adamic nature. So when individuals are ready to fear the Lord they must also be ready to open up their souls to the Lord. A closed soul to the Lord is an open soul to eternal damnation! Open up your soul now to the Lord and receive from Him all that makes for life and godliness. No one knows what might happen during the next hour.

The fear of the Lord constrains us. It constrains one from purposeful error. Many refrain from stealing, not necessarily because they are constrained by the love of the Lord, but perhaps they are afraid of going to jail. Likewise some individuals run away from immorality, not because they love the Lord, but because they do not want to contract any diseases. As long as something keeps you away, it is good, but what would happen if these things (jail and sexually transmitted diseases) are not a barrier? Will you let loose? Hence your discipleship must be Spirit driven.

A child that only trembles at the presence of the parents will certainly get off track when the parents are absent. Your fear must be divinely empowered, not physically motivated.

There was a man by the name of Nehemiah. He had a reputation for fearing the Lord. He was distinguished with much responsibility, a politician who might be equated with our modern day prime minster. That was how highly placed and influential he was. However, his testimony is a challenge to you and me, owing to the fact that he was honourable. He did not terrorize people with his position. Read what He said: "...But the former governors lived at the expense of the people and took from them food and wine, besides forty shekels of silver [a large monthly official salary]; yes, even their servants assumed authority over the people. But **I did not so because of my** [reverent] **fear of God...**" (Nehemiah 5:15 AMP).

His conduct was a product of his reverence for God. He would not misbehave. He knew that, even though people may not question him due to his position, God would definitely question him. We need to realize that none is greater than God and all of us will stand in His presence one day to give account of our lives (2 Cor 5:10).

Another man named Obadiah had the same testimony; it was recorded of him that he feared the Lord greatly. See what the Bible says: "...And Ahab called Obadiah, who was the **governor** of his house. Now Obadiah **feared the Lord greatly...**" (1 Kings 18:3 AMP). We see also that Obadiah's fear and reverence for the Lord started when he was young. Notice what he said, "**...But I, your servant, have feared and revered the Lord from my youth...**" (1 Kings 18:12 AMP).

That is why I say to every young soul that the best time to turn to Christ is in their youth! I have no doubt in me that the reason Obadiah became a governor was because he had a testimony of the fear of the Lord. Oh young people, there is no limit to your achievement and success if you would dare to have this testimony!

You remember what Joseph said when he was tempted by Potiphar's wife? He said, "...how then can I do this great wickedness, and sin against God..." (Genesis 39:9). He could not do it because he was constrained by the fear of the Lord. When you truly fear Him you will consistently seek to do His will. A man that tells his wife he loves her and goes behind her to have an affair with another woman is a liar and depicts a lack of the fear of the Lord.

Friends, you can have this testimony today if you decide to have it. The apostle, Paul, said, 'For I *decided* that while I was with you...' (1 Cor 2:2 NLT). We can always experience whatever we decide to do. Paul decided to know nothing else except Jesus Christ when he reached Corinthians, and that was exactly what happened!

The devil is not particularly scared about your desires, but he fears your godly decision! So decide now and God will help you.

4

Testimony of Purity

Keep yourself pure.

~ 1 Timothy 5:22

I once heard a message by a minister of the gospel which he titled *Living Pure in a Polluted Environment.* This message really blessed my life. You will agree with me that the whole world is polluted and as believers we are commanded by God to keep ourselves pure in this world (Lev 20:26).

The devil seems to have placed some sort of pollutant in every nook and cranny of this world. When you are outside, you will certainly see a polluted billboard. When you come inside your house and switch on the television you may likely see a picture that will pollute you. Even if you don't switch on the television you may receive a polluted letter in the post or you may be tempted to view lewd sites on the internet. There is no limit to the amount of pollution to which you can be exposed.

Sadly, the church is also polluted. The church is meant to be a city of refuge but what we see tends to be far from that. In fact I have been in some church gatherings and it seemed as though I was in a night club. Pollution!

Your Responsibility in Christianity

The apostle, Paul, told Timothy, a spiritual beloved son that he must keep himself pure (1 Tim 5:22). We need to know that for a great apostle like Paul to emphasize the need for purity in the life of Timothy, is a crucial challenge. Most youths of today think little of purity and see no reason why they should live purely. Looking closely into that Scripture in First Timothy 5:22, it says, "...Keep yourself pure..." It does not read 'God will keep you pure' neither does it say that 'Timothy's parent would keep him pure'.

Paul was letting Timothy realize that it was his responsibility to keep himself pure! Now this is where the younger generation sometimes misses it. They think someone else would make them pure. No! If you do not do it, it will never be done. So how do you keep yourself pure? Well it depends on you. You must know who you are and your weaknesses. When this is well understood, you then must enforce principles of practical discipline that will ensure your purity.

To sustain your salvation and stand in the Lord, you have to break every relationship with ungodly friends who can influence you back to your old sinful life. The Bible says, "Be not deceived: evil communications corrupt good manners" (1Cor. 15:33). If you do not disengage from these friends, it is very likely that they will drag you back, like a dog, to your own vomit. (See Amos 3:3)

You need to realize that purity is a matter of life and death. No immoral person will see God (Heb 12:14). Also if you know you were an alcoholic before you were saved, now you know you must stop; you must run away from any form of alcohol. You may need to separate yourself from every friend who may entice you back to your old way of life. Keep yourself pure. The responsibility is yours. However, God supplies adequate grace (supernatural ability).

Street Evangelism

I once met a young lady through my street evangelism. I tried to tell her about the salvation plan of God for mankind but she said, "I go to church, I am a Christian already" (Going to church does not mean you are saved). The Bible says, **"...if any man be in Christ, he is a new creature"** (2 Cor. 5:17). Most people misread that Scripture and they think it says something like this: "If anyone goes to church, he is a new creature." No! Accepting Christ gives you salvation, *not* accepting church. Make sure you are genuinely saved today. Friends, it is high time we stop playing church! The end is near. Jesus is coming soon.

Her appearance did not even look like someone that was really saved (some might say, "How did you know she was not saved?" Read Matthew 7:16, 20). In any case, I waited a bit to think about what to say to her; then her phone rang. Her conversation confirmed what I sensed in my spirit). Following her phone conversation, I asked her, "Was that your boyfriend?" Without hesitation she answered "Yes." I asked her if she knew that the Bible forbids it and also that sex before marriage is wrong---it is a sin? Oh, she got mad at me and she said "Who told you?" I answered "The Bible!" Then she replied, "What sort of Bible do you have?" I must have answered "King James Version" because she continued, "Throw it away, man, this is a new generation."

When I heard those words it was as if someone threw a rock at me. I became very sad and I asked her, "What church do you attend?" She told me the name and I asked her, "What kind of message does your pastor preach to you?" Without hesitation, she replied, "My pastor does not preach like you are preaching," and immediately she walked away. I thought to myself, "If the pastor would preach the true gospel he would have better and more lasting godly fruit."

The experience with that young lady made me very sad. I could only weep and pray for her that God would deliver her from satanic bondage.

Oh yes, we may all be tempted, but remember, "There hath no temptation taken you but such as is common to man: but God is faithful, who will not suffer you to be tempted above that ye are able; but will with the temptation also make a way to escape, that ye may be able to bear it" (1 Cor 10:13).

The Bible declares that we should, "Abstain from all appearance of evil" (1 Thess 5:22).

And again it says, "Flee (run away) also (from) youthful lusts: but follow righteousness, faith, charity, peace, with them that call on the Lord out of a pure heart" (2 Tim 2:22).

Let us see 2 Timothy 2:22 in the New Living Translation. It states plainly: "**Run** from anything that **stimulates youthful lusts**. Instead, **pursue** righteous living, faithfulness, love, and peace. **Enjoy** the companionship of those who call on the Lord with **pure** hearts."

Looking closely into these verses of the Bible, it shows us what a youth should do if he must have a testimony of purity. Firstly, he must run, he then must pursue, and then enjoy! And he must learn to say no! This tells me that as a youth there are things I must run from, there are things I must pursue and finally there are things I must enjoy doing (See Ps 133:1, Prov 27:17, 1 Tim 6:11 & 2 Tim 2:22).

When you check through the Scriptures, you will see that the young men who had a testimony of purity became great, but before their greatness, when the challenge that could have made them lose their testimony came against them, they did what the youths of this generation are failing to do. They said no! Just say no! When you say NO, you are basically running away from the trap of the devil. When you say No, it means you are saying to the devil, "Get thee behind me, Satan; I am pursuing God." Also when you say No, it means you do not enjoy the world."

Whether its drugs, just say no! Illicit sex? Just say no! Alcohol? Just say no! Masturbation? Just say no! Cigarettes? Just say no.

Joseph Said No

Genesis 39:7-13

⁷And it came to pass after these things, that his master's wife cast her eyes upon Joseph; and she said, 'Lie with me.'

⁸But he refused, and said unto his master's wife, 'Behold, my master wotteth not what is with me in the house, and he hath committed all that he hath to my hand; ⁹There is none greater in this house than I; neither hath he kept back anything from me but thee, because thou art his wife: how then can I do this great wickedness, and sin against God?'

¹⁰And it came to pass, **as she spake to Joseph day by day,** that he hearkened not unto her, to lie by her, or to be with her.

¹¹And it came to pass about this time, that Joseph went into the house to do his business; and there was none of the men of the house there within.

¹²And she caught him by his garment, saying, 'Lie with me:' and he left his garment in her hand, and fled, and got him out.

¹³And it came to pass, when she saw that he had left his garment in her hand, and was **fled** forth,

In most circumstances, men are known to be the ones to approach a lady, but in the case of Joseph, it was different. According to what we read in Genesis 39:6-13, it seems to me that Joseph was a very handsome young man, just barely eighteen years of age, looking very charming, hormones rising, adrenaline pumping (watch out because at some point in your life the hormones will rise and pump, but what will you do?)

Unlike many young people today, Joseph did not misuse his handsome appearance. You will hear them say things like, "I am eighteen, you know, and I own my body and I can do whatever I like with my body." I say to those people that it is foolishness. You do not own yourself; your body is the temple of the Holy Spirit (1 Cor 6:19). But it saddens my heart when I see people misuse their bodies.

Potiphar's wife made advances toward Joseph, not once, not twice, she lusted after Joseph, and she wanted to destroy his dreams and visions. So many young people have had their dreams destroyed by the enemy of their soul; so many destinies have been cut short due to immorality. Friends, having so many opposite-sex partners flocking around you reflects not wisdom but rather foolishness, because if you do not stop now and keep yourself pure, you may realize that your *heroes* have been reduced to *zero*.

Joseph said no to Potiphar's wife. I do not believe the young people of this generation can have a testimony of purity without saying no. And I also do not believe they can say no without Jesus Christ, and His transforming power which we receive upon salvation. This is available through the ministry of the Holy Spirit and is needed in this generation. This alone will enable anyone that is ready to say no to this world (See Zech. 4 :6).

The Holy Ghost speaking through the apostle, Paul, declares in Romans 12:1-2, "I beseech you therefore, brethren, by the mercies of God, that ye present your bodies a living **sacrifice, holy, acceptable** unto God, which is your reasonable service. And be not conformed to this world: but be ye transformed by the renewing of your mind, that ye may prove what is that good, and acceptable, and perfect, will of God."

The NLT puts it this way: **"And so, dear brothers and sisters, I plead with you to give your bodies to God because of all he has done for you. Let them be a living and holy sacrifice—the kind he will find acceptable. This is truly the way to worship him. Don't copy the behavior and customs of this world, but let God transform you into a new person by changing the way you think. Then you will learn to know God's will for you, which is good and pleasing and perfect."**

Notice it says do not conform; that means do not copy the behaviour of this world. Paul is basically telling us to say no to this world. But how do we do this? Look closely again: Paul said it is by the renewing of our minds. That is, changing the way we think. But how? Paul said it is by the transformation that comes by the reading and meditating on the word of God. Awesome!

Friends, to say no in this polluted world, you need the word of God. You must read it, drink it, chew it, meditate on it, feed on it, and give yourself wholly to it until you become the person God desires you to be.

If you are a young man, read what David wrote in Psalm 119, verse 9 to 11. I personally believe that David had a problem saying no at some point in his life, but notice what he discovered: "Wherewithal shall a young man cleanse his way? by taking heed thereto according to thy word. With my whole heart have I sought thee: O let me not wander from thy commandments. Thy word have I hid in mine heart, that I might not sin against thee."

See NLT version of Ps 119:9-11, "How can a young person stay pure? By obeying your word **(you can only obey what you know and we know the scriptures by reading the scriptures)**. I have tried hard and I find you don't let me wander from your commands. I have hidden your word in my heart that I might not sin against you." Stay close to the word. It works!

5

Testimony of Vision

*And it shall come to pass afterward, that I will pour out my spirit upon all flesh; and your sons and your daughters shall prophesy, your old men shall dream dreams, your **young men shall see visions.***

~ Joel 2:28

Vision is the mental picture of the future that is imparted upon the soul of the visionary by God. Vision makes humans relevant in the agenda of God for their generation. Anyone with a vision does not die. Though he may die physically, his work will speak loudly after he is long gone. Something invisible keeps a man with a vision moving. It impacts upon his soul a sense of urgency, and being conscious of this, he resolves never to be lazy. He moves faster and soon is ahead of his lethargic friends. He becomes a wonder, and in his light others see light. He wakes up and leaves his bed each morning because of his vision. It appears as though something of an invisible force is pushing him. He is ready to fight anyone who wants to stand against his vision. Vision, above all is auto-propelling!

A visionary is like Joseph; he never ceases to shout: I have a dream! I have a dream! He is not controlled by what goes on in the mind of his hearers. Though he is sold into a strange land or he is thrown into prison, the vision makes him jump for joy whenever he remembers it because he believes that *faithful is He that has called him —* and He who has called him, will also do it (1 Thess 5:24). He knows what the Scriptures says concerning vision in Habakkuk chapter 2 verses 2 to 3, that, "…the vision is yet for an appointed time, but at the end it shall speak, and not lie: though it tarry, wait for it; because it will surely come, it will not tarry…"

He is happy despite the challenges; in fact he becomes worried when there are no challenges as he knows all genuine divine vision must be contested by the pit of hell. So he is fully armed and prepared to wage war against the devices of the devil. He is fully aware that visions are to be fought for (See 1 Timothy 1:18). He is not ignorant of his ways; and he knows, after he has fought, he will stand.

He know that visions are better received at a young age, so he reaches out and does whatever it takes to get it. Again he obeys the prophetic words of Habakkuk that say, "I will stand upon my watch, and set me upon the tower, and will watch to see what he will say unto me, and what I shall answer when I am reproved. And the LORD answered me, and said, Write (**Why write the vision? It is because God loves details. He expects you to write all He shows and tells you VERBATIM so you do not become confused. Often people misquote God,**

so ultimately to avoid error, He wants you to write the vision, and "make it plain upon tables, that he may run that readeth it" (Habakkuk 2:1-2).

Vision is the antidote for stagnation. A man of vision is never stagnant. Though it might seem he is standing still, he knows God is at work on his behalf. Dormancy is not possible, neither is retrogression found in his dictionary. We need youths like this because often the youth appear lethargic, uninspired and visionless. They seem not to be able to see afar off! The future appears bleak. Can I bring to your attention that the major progress anyone would make and the one heaven one would recognise has to be attached to a divine vision? Without this, you are merely existing, not really living. But thanks be to God, you can become a living soul today with a revelation-vision of Christ embedded in your spirit-man.

Characteristics of Vision

From the book of Habakkuk, chapter two, we see from verses one to three that there are specific characteristics that are peculiar to vision. Look and think well on them, I trust the Holy Spirit to unveil them in a deeper manner to you. First, vision is mostly *acquired by personal determination*, that is, you will have to stand in God's presence until you receive divine instruction.

Second, God is ready when we are ready. God will answer us whenever we call upon Him (See Jer 29:11-14 & 33:3). People need to get that into their minds! Stop waiting on God; He is rather waiting for you. Draw near and you will see Him! Thirdly, it must be *written down* and well spelled out. (This talks about clarity as it is essential to every vision.)

Fourthly, you must *read* the vision *continually:* that means you must be acquainted with the vision. You should be able to give full details to anyone who asks you without missing any word! *You must also run with your vision.* You do not receive a vision just for you to go brag about or sleep. You must get to work. However, every vision is *timed,* and every vision has a time and place of manifestation! (See Ecc 3:1-8).

Vision *has a voice;* this voice is what directs the visionary. When this voice is silenced, it is as though the visionary is dead. Pray like this, "the voice of my vision shall not be silenced and every power that wants to silence the voice of my vision, die now in Jesus' name." So also, every vision requires *patience* for proper manifestation (See Heb 12:1).

Finally, every vision is tru*e to the visionary*---that is, the visionary is convinced beyond every reasonable doubt that what he has seen is real. This is where zeal, passion, dedication, sacrifice, inspiration and determination which are all crucial in order to fulfil every vision is generated.

Now While You Are Young

Being young is to be creative, innovative, productive, vibrant, explorative and resourceful. I once heard of a survey that was conducted on the levels at which an individual becomes relevant to his or her generation. It turned out that 70% started or knew what they had been called to do at a youthful age (between ages 18 and 35) and 20%

decided this between ages 35 and 50. The remaining 10% fell between the ages of 50 and 85 years.

Now look closely, the most sensitive age is between 18 and 35 years. Imagine an individual that grows out of all three age spectrums without a definite sense of direction or vision; that would be catastrophic! The individual may never amount to anything unless God intervenes. Regrettably, many have frittered away their lives like that, without being able to affect their generation. God would ask them what they did with what He gave them and I do not know what they will answer!

> Remember, "Where there is no vision **(sight, revelation, dream)**, the people perish **(regardless of their influence)**" (Prov 29:18).

Jesus: A Visionary

Jesus, at the tender age of twelve, had a vision and revelation of His future. In Luke, chapter 2, we see His parents looking for Him and we note His reply to them. Mary, His mother, said, "...Son, why hast thou thus dealt with us? Behold, thy father and I have sought thee sorrowing..." and Jesus Christ replied, "...How is it that ye sought me? Wist **(understand)** ye not that I must be about my Father's business...?" (Luke 2:48-49).

We see Jesus Christ looking after His Father's business at the age of 12. He knew it and pursued it. Do you know your Father's business? Do you have a revelation of your destiny? There are some people now that are over 28 years of age and still do not have a sense of direction. No sense of vision. When you ask them what their vision is you may hear things like, "You know God is in control." These people forget that we work in partnership with God.

God does not work in isolation. He needs our agreement. So a lack of vision may even cause us to work contrary to His will. I suggest you go to your knees and pray that God would show you the reason why He has created you. Everything in life has a purpose. You have a purpose; discover it. Nothing gives us a real sense of seriousness like a revelation of our destiny in Christ. We need to seek for it. It is for our discovery!

Daddy And Mummy, I Cannot Help It…

I once had the privilege of working with a woman whose son later became a member of the British Parliament. The mother was very happy when her son was elected to office.

I engaged in a conversation with the mother, and she said some words that I believe will stay with me for a long time. He told me about the passion of her son---that he loved politics. She said that one day, at the age of 16, the boy woke her and her husband up and said, "Daddy, mummy, I cannot help it; politics is in my blood."

The mother said to me that she and the husband were amazed. However they rendered all necessary support and guidance needed for the fulfilment of his vision. To the glory of God, May 7th 2010, this young boy, now a man, won the election of a ward and became a member of the British parliament at age 33. This is what vision can do! He saw it, ran with it, and of course, achieved it!

You see, what struck me was that at the tender age of 16 the boy already knew what was in his blood! I love that. See again. "Daddy, mummy I cannot help it; politics is in my blood." This is profound! Now let us do a bit of calculation. Subtract 33 from 16, and it gives us 17. That means he carried his vision for 17 years and I believe he has just started. The sky is the limit if he keeps running with it. In fact, I would not be surprised if, one day, he becomes the Prime Minister of Great Britain!

That brings to mind the prophetic words of Habakkuk which state, "I will stand upon my watch, and set me upon the tower, and will watch to see what he will say unto me, and what I shall answer when I am reproved. And the LORD answered me, and said, 'Write the vision, and make it plain upon tables, that he may run that readeth it (what fuel is to a vehicle is what vision is to a visionary). For the vision is yet for an appointed time, but at the end it shall speak, and not lie: though it tarry, wait for it; because it will surely come (to fulfilment), it will not (delay, though at some point it might seem delayed---in reality it will not) tarry" (Hab 2:1-3).

"Daddy, mummy I cannot help it; politics is in my blood," was what the young man said to his parents, but let us see the depth of his statement. See Leviticus, chapter 17. It says, "For the life of the flesh is in the blood..." (v. 11). Verse 14 of the same chapter says, "For it is the life of all flesh; the blood of it is for the life thereof... for the life of all flesh is the blood thereof..."

This should immediately tell you the depth of what he said to his parents. He said, "Daddy, mummy, I cannot help it; politics is in my blood." Owing to the knowledge of the Scriptures, what he meant was, "Daddy, mummy, I cannot help it; politics is my life." That is, "remove politics from me and I am as good as dead." I do not know if you understand the magnitude of what that little boy said at the age of 16. I trust God to open up your understanding. The little boy saw nothing else to live for: take away politics from him, and you might as well kill him.

It brings to mind the conversion of Paul, the apostle. However, it was recorded that Paul was "breathing out threatening." Paul's very breath was hatred and threatening! He constituted a threat to the gospel of Christ, but thank God he was converted (See Acts, chapter 9). So we can also say that the new MP (the young boy) was "breathing out politics." Now the question is: what are you breathing out? What is in your blood? What is your life? What preoccupies your thoughts? Remember that as *a man thinks in his heart so is he*! When people see you, what do they say of you?

When you mention Bill Gates you think Microsoft. When you mention Billy Graham you think worldwide evangelism, When you mention Joseph Ayodele Babalola you think African Pentecostalism, When you mention Derek Prince you think deliverance, When you mention Cassius Marcellus Clay, Jr. (Now popularly known as Muhammad Ali) you think boxing. When you mention Reinhard Bonnke you think salvation of Africans. When you mention Father Nash you think of a man of prayer. When you mention Enoch Adejare Adeboye, you think humility, holiness and Nigeria. When you mention David Olaniyi Oyedepo, you think boldness and faith; when you mention Oral Roberts, you think healing. When you mention Daniel Kolawole Olukoya you think deliverance. When you mention Martin Luther, you think Protestant reformation. When you mention George Muller you think prayer, orphanages and souls. When you mention Austin J Okocha or David Beckham you think football. When you mention Michael Jordan you think basketball. When you mention Barack Obama you think politics. When you mention Don Moen you think worship. And, in fact, when you see the flag green-white-green, no other country except Nigeria comes to mind. Likewise, the national flag of the U.S. can never be mistaken for that of England. When your name is mentioned, what thoughts run through the hearts of your fellow men?

It is disturbing to see what is evident in the lives of our youth today. Enthusiasm and exuberance is wrongly channelled toward immorality, violence, and rebellion which also morph into witchcraft, lust, pride, to mention but a few.

If you are engaged in any of these, it is my prayer that you will be delivered now in Jesus' name.

For many young people, all they know and live revolves around fashion, music and movies. All this, in itself, is not bad; but the Bible says our moderation should be known to all. When all the music you listen to and the movies you watch are carnal, they may well stimulate immorality in you and rebellion toward authority. If so, surely you are missing it. In addition, if by reason of your fashion, souls perish in hell, then you need to retrace your steps. If because of your gift(s) people are drawn away from God and are perishing, I would advise that you check yourself.

To conclude this chapter, it is important to underscore the fact that everyone has something in their blood (has a purpose to fulfil on earth), but only a few discover it in good time. May you discover yours before it is too late! Every discovery must lead to the glorification of our God! God has a plan and purpose for your life but you must seek to find it out and pursue it in a godly way.

6

Testimony of Diligence

Seest thou a man diligent in his business? he shall stand before kings; he shall not stand before mean men.

~ Proverbs 22:29

Diligence plays a vital role in the fulfilment of every vision. No vision can fulfil itself! Amongst many things that help in the fulfilment of any vision is diligence. This is the catalyst!

Have you ever wondered why you see two people with the same goals but different results? Perhaps what makes it different is the level of their diligence.

I once saw something that read like this, "WE, LIVING IN THE SAME WORLD, FIGHTING THE SAME DEVIL, BEING THE CHILDREN OF THE SAME GOD WHO IS RICH UNTO ALL THAT CALL UPON HIM, WE KNOW HE IS NOT A RESPECTER OF PERSONS. WE ARE EXPOSED TO THE SAME CHALLENGES AND OPPORTUNITIES BUT ARE GETTING DIFFERENT RESULTS! WHY?" I believe you know the reason. The rates at which human beings dedicate themselves to various issues of life are different and if the input is different. Thus, the output will never be the same. Diligence is simply an earnest, steady persistence to an undertaking---giving your all to all there is to accomplish. A diligent person is an outstanding person. He pushes well ahead of his contemporaries; he sees no barrier, and he believes he can make it if he works hard at it.

A diligent person starts small but envisions the big, hence he does things in a big way. No complacency can be found in him. He works effectively with less supervision and manages his time most efficiently. As he goes along in life, some may seem to hate him and become confused at his decisions and actions, but he is not moved. His eyes are fixed on the mark of the high calling of God.

He strives lawfully. He is such a person who is very careful about the kind of friends he keeps because he is fully aware of fire quenchers and zeal killers. His light does not mingle with darkness! No, he refuses to be tied down. His condition or his location does not determine his faithfulness because he knows that sooner or later he will assume the leadership position. He practices and understands very well the law of sacrifice.

That brings to mind a man called Jeroboam. It was recorded of him that, "...the man Jeroboam was a mighty man of valour: and Solomon, seeing the young man that he was industrious (diligent), he made him ruler over all the charge of the house of Joseph..." (1 Kings 11:28). Jeroboam was put in charge not because he was a good looking guy; neither was he put in charge because he prayed! No, because the Bible says that, "...Solomon seeing the young man that he was industrious (diligent), he made him ruler over all..." So it means that he was put in charge because he was diligent! You remember in the book of Acts of the Apostles when the apostles requested for men that would serve tables, they requested not just for men full of the Holy Ghost but also for men of honest report. What the apostles was simply saying is, "Give us spiritual men full of the Holy Ghost, but they must also have something reliable physically for the physical world to see" (See Acts 6, 7 & 8).

You do not want to be so spiritual that you are of no physical use, nor would you want to be so carnal that you are of no spiritual use. In fact, Kenneth E Hagin of blessed memory put it this way, "Some people are too heavenly minded that they are of no earthly use and some are too earthly minded and they are of no heavenly use."

What this man of God was saying is that being a Christian does not mean you should not impact your generation physically. For instance, Proverbs 14, verse 23, plainly states that, "In all labour there is profit: but the talk of the lips tendeth only to penury," This author did not mince words. He underlined the fact that laziness brings poverty both to unbelievers and God's children, alike (See Prov 24:30-34). It may interest you to know that God does not condone slothfulness.

The Bible tells us that Peter was a fisherman who was fond of labouring both night and day to provide for his household and become something in life. He was an industrious man. In fact, Jesus Christ called him while he was busy working. He never played with his profession. This was the reason while he kept fishing while men were generally supposed to be asleep. Christ did not always sleep at night; there were times when he spent the night praying (going about his Father's business) and Peter too (diligently worked at his means of livelihood). Christ must have seen his level of dedication and commitment; he knew he would not regret it if He committed His sheep into Peter's hand by and by (See John 21:15-17). The same thing goes for Elisha: Elijah called him while he was busy working, labouring with his own hands (See 1 Kings 19:19-21).

Paul: A Man of Diligence

Paul, the apostle, was also a man that was diligent. He was not disobedient to the heavenly vision; he ran with it. Little wonder that he wrote more than half of the New Testament, which is still blessing us today. It is remarkable to note that when Paul was not in prison, he was deeply involved in the work of the Lord---yet he was still laboring physically, making tents. And imprisonment did not deter his hands from working consistently, for most of his epistles were written when he was in the prison.

He said of himself, "...But in all things approving ourselves as the ministers of God, in much patience, in afflictions, in necessities, in distresses, In stripes, in imprisonments, in tumults, in labours, in watchings, in fastings; By pureness, by knowledge, by long suffering, by kindness, by the Holy Ghost, by love unfeigned..." (2 Corinthians 6:4-6).

The youth of this generation must see the need for diligence and persistence. When a youth catches the fire of diligence and runs with it in the right direction, not even the sky can be the limit.

Proverbs 12:24 AMP says that, "...The hand of the diligent will rule, but the slothful will be put to forced labor." This was exactly what happened to Jeroboam in First Kings 11:28 which we read earlier. King Solomon actually gave Jeroboam a higher responsibility and promoted him to a position of authority over others because he was very hard working and productive. This means anyone who takes pains to be diligent will definitely gain a reputation of recommendation. Because such a person has been faithful in little, he will soon be made ruler over many things. Any that are diligent when young will get that which will enable them to rule and to rest when they are old.

7

Can I Have My Dad, Please?

> "...he shall turn the heart of the fathers to the children, and the heart of the children to their fathers...
>
> ~ Malachi 4:6

I am grateful to God, not just for this book, but particularly for this unique chapter. The last thing that would cross anyone's mind about this book is a chapter about "FATHERHOOD." First of all, this is a book for the young people; but, let me add that it's not necessarily meant for youth alone; it will surely bless anyone that reads it. Secondly, Owing to the fact that I have not yet biologically fathered a child.

Now I believe this is God's wisdom at work and whatsoever is from God is above all. Yes, the author is young but my experiences have helped make me more mature. As a young man I have seen a lot. My love for God and His things have opened my eyes to the realities of life as it pertains to family, which definitely involves fatherhood and child-rearing.

Writing about what I have seen, heard, and observed will result in a story that perhaps will never end. However, I will share the content that fits into the main purpose for this chapter.

During one of our church services, I glimpsed a young boy of about eleven years of age. I had always known him and loved to play with him. However I had not seen him in a while and he now appeared so big. We played together and I teased him about his new stature and the diet which must have contributed to his size. I asked "how is your mum and dad?" He answered, "Oh, that is mum (he pointed toward where his mother sat) but dad and mum have separated."

I asked why and when and he explained. "Some months ago it happened; mum and dad separated and later came back together and then, again, separated." While he narrated the sad story, he looked so dejected and hopelessly confused! I could not but shed tears. I could look five or ten years down the line, imagining a young boy of that age growing up without a father figure.

I could see a hopeless future except God's intervention. The mother would have to work twice as hard, if anything good would come out of the young boy, I should make clear that God's grace has no limits. There are children that grow up without a father figure and still end up becoming great. Dr. Ben Carson is a good example. However this is an exceptional case. Prevention, we know, is better than cure.

The influence of a father on his family can never be overemphasized. God desires a man in every home who will direct and nurture it in the way of the Lord. A man is not just called a man because he provides financially for the house but he is called a man because he has been placed there by God to render unto the house that which is good, perfect and acceptable in the sight of God.

From the above passage we can see that God is very keen about fatherhood. It is true that the strength of a country is determined partly by the strength of the fathers in that country and that is the very reason the devil does everything in his power to destroy the family. It is true that when you smite the shepherd, the sheep will scatter.

After Eve ate the forbidden fruit and gave it also to Adam, God came down as was His custom, to fellowship with them. But when they heard God's footsteps they ran and hid themselves. See what is recorded in Genesis 3:9. It says, "And the LORD God called unto Adam (**the man**), and said unto him, Where art thou?" You know what God was saying? In essence, he was saying, "**Adam, where are you? I put you in charge of this garden.**"

This shows us that God will hold every man responsible for whatever happens in his garden (home). It will pay fathers to realize this and wake up to their responsibilities.

Wanted: Real Fathers!

What we face in the families of this generation is a fathers' problem and not so much of a youth problem. It is certain that if we can get the fathers to act in line with the word of God, we are not likely to have so many problems with the youth. Whenever you see a rebellious youth, ask the fellow where his father is; you might end up with answers like "My father is dead," "I don't know my father," "I live with my mum," "I live on my own."

Another unique category will report that their father lives at home." But when you dig deeper you will find out that, though the father is physically present, his presence is not felt owing to the fact that, he makes no contribution to family life, neither does he care about how the family is run. Hence, the children under his roof are let loose and the Devil takes advantage of his laxity.

Fathers need to be aware that there is a battle going on between them and the devil over the lives of their children. The devil is pulling; the fathers are also pulling. Any father that pulls, must pull by the Spirit of the Lord if he desires to win the contest. The fight is winnable through the help of the Holy Spirit.

If we challenge fathers to act responsibly, I can assure you that we will have a decent population of youth. Moral decadence in the life of young people is often largely a result of the decadence of fathers! The quality of the shepherd determines the state of the sheep. By the same token, the quality of the lives of fathers will determine the quality of the lives of their sons and daughters. We often voice the adage: "Like father, like son" (See Hosea 4:9). Fathers, build yourselves up spiritually, mentally, emotionally, educationally and financially. It is time to measure up to the standard God is expecting from you.

Many fathers imagine that what their children need is *"gifts."* Although, these have their own rightful place, presents or gifts must be combined with an emotional and spiritual relationship with that young person.

Mentorship

Fathers need to realize that every growing young adult needs a role model or a mentor. They need someone who will influence them. When fathers do not respond to this call, the devil will take advantage. Remember, Satan and the fleshly nature will always fill a vacuum! A Paul—Timothy relationship is needed. A Mordecai—Esther relationship is essential. A Moses—Joshua relationship is a must.

Fatherhood is a great privilege and responsibility. Edwin Louis Cole paints a vivid picture: **"Being a male is by birth but being a man is by choice, and true manhood equals Christlikeness."** An average young male wants to enjoy the privileges of marriage but runs away from its responsibility. The two go together. You see, women must use wisdom and be careful in selecting a man. They must ensure that the man with whom they intend to spend the rest of their life has a sense of responsibility and knows what biblical fatherhood means.

My heart bleeds when I see single mothers having to work longer and harder than necessary simply because the father is not responding to his duties. I can imagine the sort of pain and agony they go through in order to bring up their children. I see single mothers carrying all the responsibilities of parenthood and it is agony at times; I pray that our Lord will render help unto the single mothers.

See what the Bible says concerning a nation: **"Uprightness and right standing with God (moral and spiritual rectitude in every area and relation) elevate a nation, but sin is a reproach to any people (family)**

(Proverbs 14:34). You will agree with me that what makes up a nation is multiple families.

Much has been given to every father; hence, much is expected (See Prov 29:15).

8

Testimony of Stewardship

"...and he served him: and he made him..."

~ Genesis 39:4

Another testimony everybody—particularly the young adult—needs to possess is that of stewardship. By this I mean that one must possess the ability to serve. It is in service that we are tested, trained, and made.

This is clearly seen in the life of Joseph. Though he had a great destiny and many prophecies had gone ahead of him, these were not substitute for service. He was not made until he had served. The stewardship qualities and testimony did not start at Potiphar's house. His father had trained and taught him the benefit of stewardship.

Jesus the Servant

Jesus said, "And whosoever of you will be the chiefest, shall be servant of all. For even the Son of man came not to be ministered unto, but to minister and to give his life a ransom for many" Mark 10:44-45.

Here we see Jesus changing the mindset of his disciple and also disclosing His own mission to them. There had been a fight amongst the disciples about who would be the greatest. In order to settle it, Jesus changed the order from what they knew. He told them if you want to be the greatest, then you must be ready to be a servant. You must possess a stewardship mentality, you must not see yourself as the boss, rather you must serve others. To the disciples this sounded like a paradox but he finished the topic by speaking about himself.

He gave a picture of himself that he was amongst them as a servant. Though he was their master, he would not lord it over them, and he would not enforce, neither rule them in an oppressive manner but he was a servant.

He who must be great must be ready to serve. It is a great thing when men serve.

This is what I mean by service: being at the disposal of others. It is allowing people to use you so to speak. I love to think of it like this: "If you do not serve others, no one will serve you". I must make it clear that this sort of stewardship is not that of slavery as it is something that is done willingly, because it is you laying down your life voluntarily.

It Is a Seed

One of the scripture that has had a great impact on me and help shape my destiny is Galatians 6:7. It reads: "Be not deceived; God is not mocked: for whatsoever a man soweth, that shall he also reap". I love this scripture for several reasons. It is a scripture that no one – including atheists – can deny its validity. Some call it the law of karma.

It is a scripture that made me see everything I do as a seed. It specifically made me realize that serving others is a seed. By this scripture, I came to a conclusion that serving others is not a waste of time neither is it a waste of my resources. It is clear that whatever I sow I shall reap. In a way then, I determine what I reap. How do I do that? By sowing the right things!

That means there will be people to serve me if I serve others now. This is the truth I endeavour to let the people around me to see: you are helping yourself when you serve others.

What Happens

There are many things that happen when we serve. It is in service that we acquire experience. You can easily substitute for anything, but not experience.

Experience is something you learn "hands-on". You have to be there to catch it. You see, even though God has a calling for every one of his children, he would still require each one to learn (serve). In service the experience needed for the call is acquired.

There are many examples in the scripture. First, David, he was called as a king and physically anointed for it but he did not possess the "know-how". He did not possess what it takes to run a nation. Leading sheep is different from leading people. It is actually easier to lead a sheep than it is to lead human beings!

Because of this God had to send him to serve under Saul. Whilst he was serving, he was observing how things are done in the palace and how a king should conduct himself. The conduct of a king is different from a shepherd boy, the mental shift had to take place and that would only happen as he observed Saul. Anointing would not teach him that, he had to see it to know it.

There are those with genuine dreams and vision but they lack adequate experience perhaps because they have not served long enough for the acquisition of the needed skill. You can not be in a hurry to gather experience, it comes with time. My advice for you is that do not be too hasty to run, ponder very well if you have adequate experience. A graduate doctor is not considered safe – though he went to the university to learn – until he has served under the supervision of an experienced doctor.

Now that you are young, gather the necessary experience so you will not suffer in the future.

Secondly, Elisha, he had a genuine call into the prophetic ministry, but he still had to serve Elijah – his master. This is due to so many reasons. He needed to know how the prophetic ministry operates; he needed to know how to deliver a prophetic message. He had to learn how to sharpen his spiritual senses.

Your vision may be real, but lack of adequate experience would make it look unreal as though God never called you. This is happening to so many young ministers. The call is genuine, but lack commensurate experience and this is due to pride and impatience.

Habits

Habits either make or break us. As we gather experience during service, we also pick up necessary habits that are required for the future. During service, we learn new habits and drop bad ones. There are the profiting habits one needs to imbibe and there are the demoting ones that must be dropped.

Avoiding Leadership Error

One of the major things that happen when we serve is the opportunity to perfect or do things in a better way when our time comes. Whatever area it is God has given you the privilege to serve, you will surely see some things that are probably wrong (this is not the time to pass a judgement neither is it time to be critical rather, it is the time for you to take note so as to avoid the same mistake when your time of manifestation comes)

Elisha and David would have seen something wrong in the administration or leadership style of their masters, it would be unjust to make mockery of their masters, but what I believe what they did was to avoid such errors.

Above All

The culmination of this is that having been given to stewardship, if you have served at the right proportion as God would require from you, then you would be able to face the challenges and responsibilities that the future holds. You will be better equipped for the future.

For instance, a young man who served under a godly father/husband would know how to be a godly husband/husband when that phase of his life begins to open.

Above all there is an eternal reward for stewards, "And, behold, I come quickly; and my reward is with me, to give every man according as his work shall be" Revelation 22:12.

9

Scriptures for Meditation

Meditate upon these things; give thyself wholly to them; that thy profiting may appear to all.

~ 1 Timothy 4:15)

In this chapter, some Scriptures have been provided for your meditation. There is tremendous power in meditation. Sometimes we read the Bible, but, you see, reading the Bible may not produce your desired result. However, when you meditate on what you have read, your progress is bound to manifest itself.

Meditation involves active, careful and purposeful thinking. It is the medium whereby God's words get down into our spirit.

God specifically spoke to Joshua, but I believe the word was not just for Joshua but for us too. Remember that often what God says to one, He says to all. Joshua was a man of like passion as we are. The LORD told him in Joshua 1:8: "This book of the law (the word of God) shall not depart out of thy mouth (that means confession); but thou shalt meditate (imagine, ponder, utter it) therein day and night, that thou mayest observe to do according to all that is written therein: for then thou shalt make thy way prosperous, and then thou shalt have good success." Do you notice something here? Meditation is what gives you the ability to obey God! Look at it again, it says, "…that thou mayest observe to do according to all that is written therein…" When you meditate, you observe and, when you observe, you do. You see, it is a trend: Meditation-Observation-Doing!

When the final result is success, be it financial, academic, spiritual, or marital success, you are set for it. Hence for any of us to fulfil our destiny, we must devote ourselves to meditation.

Solomon knew how to do this very well. It was recorded in the book of Proverbs, chapter 24, how he got answers to some worrisome questions.

Proverbs 24:30-34

[30]I went by the field of the slothful, and by the vineyard of the man void of understanding;

[31]And, lo, it was all grown over with thorns, and nettles had covered the face thereof, and the stone wall thereof was broken down.

[32]Then I saw, and *considered* it well: I looked upon it, and received instruction.

[33]Yet a little sleep, a little slumber, a little folding of the hands to sleep:

³⁴So shall thy poverty come as one that travelleth; and thy want as an armed man

In verse 32 we saw how he received an answer: it was by meditation. It reads like this, "...Then I *(Solomon)* saw, and considered *(meditated upon)* it well: I looked upon it, and received instruction (answers)."

Hence, anyone can receive instruction if we will take time to meditate. Someone rightly said, praying is talking to God and meditation is God talking back to you. Meditation involves being quiet and that is where people miss it. So many people never quiet down so God can talk to them. The Bible commands a believer to study to be quiet (1 Thessalonians 4:11). To hear God speak to us, we must be ready to do much listening and meditating.

That is the reason for this chapter and providing these scriptures; not just to read but to ponder them deeply.

Job 29:4

As I was in the days of my youth, when the secret of God was upon my tabernacle;

Job 33:25

His flesh shall be fresher than a child's: he shall return to the days of his youth

Psalm 25:7

Remember not the sins of my youth, nor my transgressions: according to thy mercy remember thou me for thy goodness' sake, O LORD.

Psalm 71:5

For thou art my hope, O Lord GOD: thou art my trust from my youth.

Psalm 71:17

O God, thou hast taught me from my youth: and hitherto have I declared thy wondrous works.

Psalm 103:5

Who satisfieth thy mouth with good things; so that thy youth is renewed like the eagle's.

Psalm 110:3

Thy people shall be willing in the day of thy power, in the beauties of holiness from the womb of the morning: thou hast the dew of thy youth.

Psalm 127:4

As arrows are in the hand of a mighty man; so are children of the youth

Psalm 129:2

Many a time have they afflicted me from my youth: yet they have not prevailed against me.

Pro 5:18

Let thy fountain be blessed: and rejoice with the wife of thy youth.

Ecclesiastes 11:9-10

Rejoice, O young man, in thy youth; and let thy heart cheer thee in the days of thy youth, and walk in the ways of thine heart, and in the sight of thine eyes: but know thou, that for all these things God will bring thee into judgment

Therefore remove sorrow from thy heart, and put away evil from thy flesh: for childhood and youth are vanity.

Ecclesiastes 12:1

Remember now thy Creator in the days of thy youth, while the evil days come not, nor the years draw nigh, when thou shalt say, I have no pleasure in them.

Jeremiah 3:4

Wilt thou not from this time cry unto me? My father, thou art the guide of my youth.

Jeremiah 22:21

I spake unto thee in thy prosperity; but thou saidst, I will not hear. This hath been thy manner from thy youth, that thou obeyedst not my voice.

Jeremiah 48:11

Moab hath been at ease from his youth, and he hath settled on his lees, and hath not been emptied from vessel to vessel, neither hath he gone into captivity: therefore his taste remained in him, and his scent is not changed.

Lamentations 3:27

It is good for a man that he bear the yoke in his youth.

Ezekiel 16:43

Because thou hast not remembered the days of thy youth, but hast fretted me in all these things; behold, therefore I also will recompense thy way upon thine head, saith the Lord GOD: and thou shalt not commit this lewdness above all thine abominations. Ezekiel 23:3

And they committed whoredoms in Egypt; they committed whoredoms in their youth: there were their breasts pressed, and there they bruised the teats of their virginity.

Joel 2:28

And it shall come to pass afterward, that I will pour out my spirit upon all flesh; and your sons and your daughters shall prophesy, your old men shall dream dreams, your young men shall see visions.

Malachi 2:15 (New Living Translation)

Didn't the LORD make you one with your wife? In body and spirit you are his. And what does he want? Godly children from your union. So guard your heart; remain loyal to the wife of your youth.

1 Timothy 4:12 (New Living Translation)

Don't let anyone think less of you because you are young. Be an example to all believers in what you say, in the way you live, in your love, your faith, and your purity.

10

Christ in View

Looking for that blessed hope, and the glorious appearing of the great God and our Saviour Jesus Christ.

~ Titus 2:13

While we look forward with hope to that wonderful day when the glory of our great God and Savior, Jesus Christ, will be revealed.

~ Titus 2:13 NLT

Awaiting and looking for the [fulfillment, the realization of our] blessed hope, even the glorious appearing of our great God and Savior Christ Jesus (the Messiah, the Anointed One),

~ Titus 2:13 AMP

Looking Forward

Whenever a man and a woman are about to be joined together as husband and wife, they both earnestly look forward to that day. To others, that day may be insignificant but to the couple, that day is very important and perhaps will go down in their diaries as one of their most memorable days.

They individually watch eagerly for that day. All protocols are observed and they both ensure that nothing will shift their focus. Maximum preparation is made so as to make full use and benefit of that day. Though the wedding ceremony itself will not take a whole day, the joy should abide with them forever.

This is exactly what Paul is saying to Titus, a beloved son. The apostle, Paul, establishes the fact for a diligent and thorough expectation of our Lord Jesus Christ. Paul called that day a blessed day and a glorious day. This is a day in which crowns of righteousness will be given to all that love His appearing.

It is a day of reckoning, a day of joy for some and of sorrow for others. Some will hear: "Well done, thou good and faithful servant: thou hast been faithful over a few things, I will make thee ruler over many things: enter thou into the joy of thy lord…" (Mathew 25:21). While others will be rebuked by the Lord (Matthew 25:26).

The Young Soul

Oh, you young at heart, hear what the Lord is saying to you. The time of youth is the time to fly to Christ. Youth is the converting time. Though many challenges may becloud your soul, now is truly the hour for your salvation; now is the time to live with Christ in view!

Don't let the excitement of youth cause you to forget your Creator. Honour Him in your youth before you grow old and say, "Life is not pleasant anymore" (Ecc 12:1 NLT). The time of youth is a vital and sensitive period. It must be used for, with, and in the Lord. When individuals pass that stage unsaved, their life patterns are usually set and they do not wish to change. The majority of older folks that are saved now, embraced salvation when young. They came to the knowledge of the saving grace of Christ when they were still pliable.

The patience of the Lord is to give us opportunity for salvation. Now is the time to possess your soul. Watch lest the day of the Lord come upon you unawares. Be well prepared!

Oh, you may say in your heart that youth is the time to eat, drink, play and be merry. You may think that youth is the time to engage in worldly pleasures, but I say to you that youth is the time to fly to Christ. The only safe place to be is in Christ. If you are not saved you are certainly not safe! In His presence there is fullness of joy. The pleasure in the world is but for a little while. However, when you fly to Christ, there are pleasures forever. You enjoy a safety in your soul and an assurance of eternal life. Christ will show you the path of life. (Ps 16:11). There is a way that seems right in your eyes but the end is the way of death. (Prov 14:12).

So arise, awake from the dead you that are sleeping and Christ shall give you light.

Whether or not we shall be joyful at the time of the Lord's appearing depends upon our relationship with God. We must make our calling and election sure! Taking our salvation lightly is a doctrine for superficial believers. It is the doctrine of devils. We are told to work out our salvation with fear and trembling and that only those that endure to the end shall be saved. (See Philippians 2:12 and Matthew 24:13).

Living Soberly, Righteously And Godly

You see, the apostle, Paul, showed us how to get ourselves ready so that we might be happy when the Lord returns.

The Holy Spirit speaking through Paul said that believers, "…should live **soberly**, righteously, and godly, in this present world…" (Titus 2:12).

What was he trying to teach us? Before I seek to explain what he meant, we need to realize that as human beings we have three major relationships. First, we have a relationship with ourselves, second, we have a relationship with others and last, we have a relationship with God. All these must be balanced.

You cannot claim to love God when you hate your neighbour; neither is it possible if you hate yourself!

Living soberly is to live discreetly and moderately. We must be content to live a self-restricted life! Soberness is in regard to ourselves. We can read Titus 2:12, "...we should live soberly (**moderately**)..." In Philippians 4:5, the Bible says, "Let **YOUR** moderation be known unto all men...." You see, it is *your* moderation!

On the other hand, righteous living here, "...**righteously**, and godly, in this present world..." (Titus 2:12), is dealing with our relationship with other people. Finally, the apostle also points out that believers, "...should live **godly**, in this present world...." Godliness here is basically our relationship with God.

Therefore Paul is simply saying that anyone who claims to have Christ in view must live a God-expressing and flesh-restricting life. God's character should be expressed and magnified through our lives as believers.

Denying Ungodliness And Worldly Lust

Thus, as we are taught by the grace of God to live soberly, righteously and godly in this present evil world, Paul makes us to understand that certain things must also be denied.

Titus 2:12 says, "Teaching us that, denying ungodliness and worldly lusts...." The Holy Spirit here is the Teacher— teaching and empowering us through the grace of God to flee the lusts of the flesh, and the lusts of the eyes, and the pride of life.

Thus verse 12 of Titus 2 is incomplete without verse 11: "For the grace of God that bringeth salvation hath appeared to all men, teaching us that, denying ungodliness and worldly lusts...."

Worldly lusts are fleshly expressions that find satisfaction in this world. Ungodliness is the human failure to express God. All these must be denied so as to glorify God in our bodies: "For all that is in the world, the lust of the flesh, and the lust of the eyes, and the pride of life, is not of the Father, but is of the world. And the world passeth away, and the lust thereof: but he that doeth the will of God abideth forever" (1 John 2:16-17).

You have been bought with a price. Do not waste the Blood of Christ. Prepare, our Lord is coming soon. That which you are doing, do quickly!

A Prayer for the Youth

My Father who is in heaven, I magnify Your name. Your kingdom come and Your will be done here on earth as it is in heaven. Father, I pray for myself as a youth and for all the young people of the nations of the earth. Please strengthen us, empower us so as to lead godly lives in this perverse, immoral, demonic and satanic generation.

Forgive us, O Lord, of misguided youthful exuberance. Forgive us, O Lord, of every hidden sin of the heart. Though Amaziah did what was right in Your sight, it is recorded in the Scriptures that he did it with an imperfect heart. Father, we ask for forgiveness of anything we have done that seemed right in our sight, accepted among men but had no reward at Your Judgement Seat. Father, we do not want to be wise in our own eyes, but we want to trust in You with all of our hearts and to acknowledge You in all of our ways. We realize that there is a generation, (which may be the current one) that is pure in its own eyes and yet is not washed from its filthiness.

Also, Father, I know that this generation curses its fathers and does not bless its mothers. This generation is proud and lofty and its eyelid is lifted up. It is a generation that thinks so little of You, my mighty God, the Creator of heavens and earth.

They are a foolish generation that have said in their hearts that there is no God. But I know that You reign and rule in the affairs of mankind. Father, I desire that You will grant us Your Holy Spirit so as to lead, guide and protect us from the schemes of darkness. I pray that by Your power You will keep us from that evil one. We do not want You to take us away from the earth now because we have works to do for You but we want a hedge to be built around us like a wall of fire so that every evil launched at us by the kingdom of darkness will have no choice but to be rendered ineffective and void. Also, because You are the one that works in us both to will and to do of Your good pleasures, we desire that You will change our rebellious hearts and give us hearts of flesh that seek to do Your will at all points and at whatever cost. Make us see that we are nothing without You because indeed a branch cannot bear fruit except it abide in the vine. We pray that You, Father God, would open our eyes to see that we must stop engaging ourselves in fruitless efforts though they may appear good.

Father, I also pray, as You have shown me from Your word that as young people, we have two main functions: We must be a source of joy and protection to our generation. So then, Father, I pray that as arrows are in the hand of a mighty man, so we shall be in Your hand. I pray that You shall use us mightily so as to enforce Your authority here on earth and live in dominion over the world, Satan, sin and flesh, hereby bringing glory and joy to You. Having done all, we shall stand. And Father, I pray that You will stamp eternity in our eyes so we will not lose focus of the real thing which is Christ in us, the hope of glory. I pray that we shall not trade our glory for that of this world because You told us not to love the world and the things in the world because all that is in the world, the lust of the eyes, the lust of the flesh and the pride of life are not of You. We know that this world is reserved for fire and all that is therein shall melt with fervent heat. Lord, this I pray, that You will stamp eternity on our eyes. If You will show us visions and dreams, Father, please do, for what really shall it profit a man to gain the whole world and lose his soul? Or what can a man give in exchange for his soul?

As it is written in Your word: if a man dies shall he live again? No! Father, we pray that You put in us the ability to value and cherish our souls, to know they belong to You and that they must go back to You. We long for a genuine experience of redemption, as it seems that many so called believers are living a superficial life. We have not really experienced You like our fathers did: men like Joseph Ayo Babalola, Kenneth Hagin, Evan Roberts, Father Nash and Charles G. Finney. Father, we pray for a definite touch: unforgettable and indelible.

Moses could never forget the burning bush; Paul will never forget the voice that came to him on his way to Damascus; Joseph will never forget his dream; Jacob will never forget his permanent hip injury as he wrestled with You; Joseph Ayo Babalola will never forget his divine visitation at 3:00 a.m. on the seventh day of his dry fast (no food, no water). All these we know come with a price, so we ask for the grace to pay the price to experience You. This is what we desire and thirst for. So help us, in Jesus name Amen.

I recommend that you do not just say this prayer but please say it meditatively so that it truly permeates your inner man.

Prayer Points

Bible Reading:

Luke 1:80, 2:25. Malachi 3:1-3, Eph. 1:17-19, 3:14-20, Prov. 23:18. Heb. 1:9. Deut. 28:13. Ps. 113:5-8. Ps 27:6. 1 Cor. 6, Gal. 5

1. Father Lord, may I not regret my youthful stage when I am old in the name of Jesus.
2. O Lord, anoint my destiny afresh in the name of Jesus.
3. My destiny is attached to God; therefore I decree that I can in the name of Jesus.
4. I reject every satanic alternative for my destiny in the name of Jesus.
5. Destiny swallowers vomit my destiny in the name of Jesus.
6. I refuse to accept satanic substitutes for my destiny in the name of Jesus.
7. Destiny thieves release me now in the name of Jesus.
8. I shall fulfil my divine destiny whether the Devil likes it or not in the name of Jesus.
9. Father, make me a person of integrity in the name of Jesus.
10. Put the love for purity in my heart in the name of Jesus.

11. Change my heart, O Lord; make me be like you in the name of Jesus
12. May the vibrancy of the Holy Spirit overshadow me now in the name of Jesus.
13. May I increase in wisdom, knowledge and understanding in the name of Jesus.
14. My future is bright in the name of Jesus.
15. Every spirit of rebellion in me, die now in the name of Jesus.
16. Any power manipulating my destiny, die now in the name of Jesus.
17. Every power, spirit and personality saying no to my moving forward, die now by fire in the name of Jesus.
18. Amen and Amen, Jesus shall reign all over my destiny.
19. I receive power to mount up with wings as an eagle in the name of Jesus.
20. Every infidelity in me, die now in the name of Jesus.
21. I break and loose myself from every evil soul tie covenant in the name of Jesus.
22. Oh Lord, make me a man of Your word in the name of Jesus.
23. My Lord, make me a man of my word in the name of Jesus.
24. I shall be the head and not the tail in the name of Jesus.
25. Every form of barrenness, (put the area where you are experiencing lack, e.g. spiritual, emo-

tional, financial, academic, marital) in my life, be consumed by the fire of the Holy Spirit in the name of Jesus.

26. Holy Ghost fire, burn continually in me in the name of Jesus.
27. Refiner's fire, refine my vessel, make it fit for the master's use in the name of Jesus.
28. I refuse to be a vessel of wrath in the name of Jesus.
29. I shall be a vessel of mercy in the name of Jesus.
30. May fuller's soap wash away every dirtiness in me in the name of Jesus.
31. Pray now in the Holy Ghost for 20 minutes (Write whatever comes to your spirit).
32. May the eyes of my understanding open now in the name of Jesus.
33. I receive the revelation vision of Jesus Christ in the name of Jesus.
34. I receive the end-time reality revelation in the name of Jesus.
35. I shall end my course joyfully in the name of Jesus.
36. I shall not be a cast away in the name of Jesus.
37. The Spirit of the fear of the Lord fall upon me now in the name of Jesus.
38. The quickening power of the Holy Spirit fall upon my life now in the name of Jesus.
39. Create in me a clean heart, O Lord, in the name of Jesus.

40. I receive gifts that will make a way for me in the name of Jesus.
41. Through my life souls shall be saved in the name of Jesus.
42. I shall be a responsible father, mother, son, daughter (put your position) in the name of Jesus.
43. I receive the power to maintain the integrity of the Kingdom of God that is at work in me in the name of Jesus.
44. I receive the grace needed to pay the price for my glorious destiny in Christ in the name of Jesus.
45. My spiritual eyes, open now in the name of Jesus.
46. My spiritual mouth, open now and begin to speak forth the mystery of God in the name of Jesus.
47. My spiritual ears, begin to hear things that will move my life forward in the name of Jesus.
48. I shall be celebrated, I will not be tolerated in the name of Jesus.
49. I will be a blessing to generations yet unborn in the name of Jesus.
50. Pray again in the Holy Ghost and, afterwards, praise God in your own local dialect.
51. Prayer for Salvation - See next page.

Prayer for Salvation

Except a human is born again he will never and can never see the kingdom of God. Salvation is mandatory for anyone that desires to enter into the kingdom of God. Without salvation no one will see God. You need to be saved from the wrath of God that is coming upon this disobedient generation. Now say this prayer…

> Heavenly Father, I come to You in the name of Your Son Jesus. Your word says that, "And it shall come to pass, that whosoever shall call on the name of the Lord shall be saved." Act 2:21.

> I am calling on You now. I pray and desire that You come into my heart now and be my Lord and Saviour according to Your word which says, "That if thou shalt confess with thy mouth the Lord Jesus, and shalt believe in thine heart that God hath raised him from the dead, thou shalt be saved.

For with the heart man believeth unto righteousness; and with the mouth confession is made unto salvation." Romans 10:9-10. I do that now, I believe in my heart that Jesus Christ was raised from the dead on the third day and I confess with my mouth that He is Lord. I ask that You forgive me of my sins and cleanse me with Your blood. This I ask for in Jesus name. Amen

Having said this prayer, I believe you are now saved. Look for a Bible-believing and -teaching church that will enhance your growth in the knowledge and grace of God.

Prayer for Baptism in the Holy Ghost

Power is needed to run the race which you have just begun. Jesus Christ told His disciples never to go out and do anything until they had been endued with power from on high.

The power is made available by the ministry of the Holy Spirit, with an evidence of speaking in tongues. God desires that you should be baptized and speak in the heavenly language, He gives you the utterance but you will have to open your mouth and speak out boldly those words as you are given utterance.

You do not have to understand what the words mean. Just speak out as you receive it. Say this prayer with all genuineness of heart.

> Father Lord, I come to You in the name of Jesus Christ and I ask You to fill me with the Holy Spirit now with the evidence of speaking with tongues, because You said in Your word that, "...If ye then, being evil, know how to give good gifts unto your children: how much more shall your heavenly Father give the Holy Spirit to them that ask him...." Luke 11:13.
>
> I also know from Your word that, "...everyone who asks receives, and he who seeks finds, and to him who knocks it will be opened..."Matthew 7:8 NKJV. Holy Spirit, rise up within me now as I begin to praise

God. I am ready and fully expect to speak in tongues now as You give me utterance in the name of Jesus Christ. Amen.

Now lift up your hands and begin to praise God. Then speak those words as they come to you now in Jesus' name. Amen

Having received the baptism of the Holy Ghost with the evidence of speaking with tongues, you must constantly speak those words. I recommend a daily speaking.

www.ingramcontent.com/pod-product-compliance
Lightning Source LLC
Chambersburg PA
CBHW052100070526
44584CB00017B/2267